# THE CUSTOMER HAS CHANGED

# HAVE YOU?

## HOW TO SELL TO THE
## 21st CENTURY
## BUYER

Bill Hart

authorHOUSE°

*AuthorHouse™*
*1663 Liberty Drive*
*Bloomington, IN 47403*
*www.authorhouse.com*
*Phone: 1 (800) 839-8640*

*Published by AuthorHouse 12/12/2017*

*ISBN: 978-1-5462-1054-2 (sc)*
*ISBN: 978-1-5462-1046-7 (hc)*
*ISBN: 978-1-5462-1047-4 (e)*

*Library of Congress Control Number: 2017914930*

*Print information available on the last page.*

*Any people depicted in stock imagery provided by Thinkstock are models, and such images are being used for illustrative purposes only.*
*Certain stock imagery* © *Thinkstock.*

*This book is printed on acid-free paper.*

*Because of the dynamic nature of the Internet, any web addresses or links contained in this book may have changed since publication and may no longer be valid. The views expressed in this work are solely those of the author and do not necessarily reflect the views of the publisher, and the publisher hereby disclaims any responsibility for them.*

# Contents

This book is dedicated to my father, Joseph W. Hart, Jr. who exemplified Customer Aligned Selling™ in running his insurance agency. He taught me to focus on the customer and their desired outcome; then sales will follow.

Many thanks to my family, mentors, and friends who encouraged me to start my business. My clients have had a big impact on the development of this curriculum and have had input on the progression of this book.

To my wife, Varina, for encouraging me to pursue what I do best.

Thanks to Jeffery Gitomer, who encourages trainers to begin writing and publish a book.

"Bill's focus on understanding where the buyer is in the buying process and dealing with the issue of risk has been very helpful to our teams in achieving their sales goals. This book is a great resource for senior sales leaders who see their sales team facing headwinds and are seeking new answers to the cause of the struggle."

Stan Viner – General Manager - Sales, Jack Henry & Associates

"Bill Hart understands and practices what so many sales people fail to grasp. Selling is more about "synching" than "selling." This book teaches you how to synch up with your customer to achieve the win/win which is vital for true long-term success."

Scott Watson CFA, MBA – Director, UAB
Center for Sales Leadership

Principal, The C=C Bond Group

"Bill Hart led our sales team through the Customer Aligned Selling course. This is the best course to come along in a number of years. Customer Aligned Selling provided our team the skill set to partner with users for a desired outcome. The information was easy to understand and apply. Our sales staff enjoyed the course and improved their performance in face-to-face selling, inside (phone) sales and lead management. (post conference follow-up). Bottom line – it was effective at increasing our focus on helping our customers achieve their desired outcomes."

Bruce Shorer – Vice President – Sales,
Occupational Health Dynamics (retired)

"Bill is the consummate sales professional and is the best, most effective sales trainer that I have met. Customer Aligned Selling is based upon science and thus is a repeatable process."

Brunson White - Senior Vice President, Alagasco
(retired), Technology Consultant

"As a new sales rep, the Customer Aligned Selling process enabled me to immediately engage the prospect in relevant conversations, identify his buying criteria while making it less stressful for me as a new sales rep and making it a productive conversation for the prospective buyer. I exceeded my first year sales goals using this process. The whole company is now utilizing Customer Aligned Selling."

James Palmer – Sales Representative, Taylor Sales & Service

"Amen! This process works."

Jimmy Palmer – President, Taylor Sales &Service

"In this book, you will find lots of great tools to help sales reps improve their understanding of how their product and services impact business drivers and how to align with the customer's buying criteria."

James Justice – Chapter President, Truth At Work

"Customer Aligned Selling changed my whole thinking on our sales processes. We were selling from our perspective and not to the buyer's perspective. All new sales reps are required to go through the Customer Aligned Selling training. Whole Brain˙ Thinking had a significant impact on how we now view and interact with our customers."

Daniel Gallegly – Owner, Valpak Alabama

## Selling is a Beauty Contest

Selling is a beauty contest, not a race. Unfortunately, many sales reps and sales leaders focus on their goals, their quota, and making the numbers in the forecasted time frame, thus creating the sense of a race. This race approach is very seller-centric, not customer-centric which is a 20th century approach vs. 21st century approach. According to a 2015 Salesforce.com study, 82% of sellers are out of sync with their customers.

Think about a beauty contest. The contestants are not in a rush. They focus on each stage of the contest and give their best effort. They take their time and focus on the judges, not their own desires. The ones who win the contest focus not only on the rules, but intently on the judges. The best contestants research whether the judges have judged other contests and how they judged, i.e. who won and why.

A beauty contest is a great metaphor for the sales process. A sales organization needs not only to understand what the customer wants (the rules of the contest), but also why rules are important, and what specific personal criteria the buyer will be using to make his or her decision. A critical question is, "What evidence does the customer need to see to make his/her decision?" Another way to ask that question is, "Mr. Customer, what do you need to see to know our offering is the best or right decision?"

Every beauty contest has stages, as do buying processes. There are different criteria for each stage of the contest. With a buyer, there are stages of needs, evaluation and commitment. Specific criteria are used to evaluate each stage. In a beauty contest, the judges will have different experiences and different personal motives for how they score. The same goes with buyers. They bring their past experiences and personal motives to the buying process. As a seller, should you not know what they are?

An effective beauty contestant is deliberate, calculated, and always in touch with the judges. She does not have her agenda as the main focus. Instead, she is focusing on what the judges expect and caters to them. Unfortunately, in most sales situations, the seller is focused on themselves, their products, and is rushing toward the close without ever slowing down enough to truly understand the buyer's buying criteria.

In the last 15 years, the world of sales has greatly changed, making the metaphor of a beauty contest even more pertinent. The Internet has changed the entire paradigm of selling. The buyer or customer is now empowered. The customer can do research on your product and services, get feedback on your company, and even get pricing without the input of the sales executive. The playing field of sales has forever changed. Have you adjusted to the new playing field? Has your sales team adapted? Have your internal operations conformed to the 21st century buyer? Are you still using sales techniques birthed in the 1990's? Consultative selling is no longer enough. The customer demands more!

Are you prepared to give more?

This book was written to give an overview of how companies and individuals buy in the 21st century, and what it takes to be an effective sales organization, and an effective solution provider. My goal is to give sales leaders a description of what Customer Aligned Selling™ is and where to begin implementing the transformation within your organization or your personal selling practices. This book is a compilation of best practices gleaned from research, training companies, sales books, psychology, and the science of the brain, combined with 30 years of sales experience. I will quote from authors such as Jeffery Gitomer, Neil Rackham, Ph.D., Howard Stevens, Ph.D., Michael Bosworth, John R. Holland, and Kevin Davis. I will refer to practices of training companies like Axiom Sales Force Development, Customer Centric Selling, Wilson Learning, and Chally Assessments.

I call myself a *Sales Chiropractor.* Just as a medical chiropractor adjusts and aligns the human body, I help sales organizations adjust and become aligned with the way their customers prefer to buy. The result is reduced sales cycles, increased revenues, contented salespeople, and loyal customers. Aligning your sales strategy and implementation with how your customer wants to buy works - just ask your customers. Customer Aligned Selling is a concept as old as antiquity; "Treat others as you would have them treat you."

Almost all sales training until the 1990s (there are a few sales trainers who have not followed the crowd) was about learning techniques to manipulate the customer into buying. In the late 1980s through 1990s, even the idea of Solution or Consultative Selling was for the purpose of making a sale. Customer Aligned Selling's driving force is to help the customer achieve their desired outcome throughout the complete sales process. It is customer focused, not sales effort focused!

In today's economy, organizations face many challenges in terms of delivering the sales numbers on a quarterly basis. For many, the focus has been on doing whatever it takes to get the customer to buy. Those "do whatever it takes" tactics are delivering a declining rate of return, and senior managers are wondering why competitors are easily taking market share. Executives assume that the competitor's offering must be the lowest price. Have your company's sales stagnated? Could you be losing market share because your competitors have made the shift from the traditional sales model to Customer Aligned Selling™?

> The buying process and desired outcome are the driving factors in how and why a buyer selects a vendor.

Customer Aligned Selling is where all sales efforts are initiated with the customer's <u>buying process and outcome</u> being the driving factor in the sales process. Customer Aligned organizations understand that operations and sales cannot be separate silos. They have changed the role of marketing from being an extension of operations or manufacturing to the first connection with the customer - hearing what the customer truly wants or needs.

I repeat myself in this book, but for a good reason. The old Latin saying is "Repetitio est mater studiorum." Translated, it means "Repetition is the mother of all learning." I present the same truth from many different perspectives with the hope that you, the reader, will go beyond understanding to application. I have worked with many sales reps and senior sales executives who have told me "I already know that." As Jeffrey Gitomer, the famous sales trainer and author, says about knowledge versus application:

> *"It is not what you know or think you believe, but how you act that demonstrates what you believe. It is not what you know, but how good you are at what you know that determines your success."*

As a sales leader or senior manager, I encourage you to go beyond just working "in" your business, and that you take time to work "on" your business. Regularly evaluate your go to market strategy and what is working in the field. Spend time on sales calls and evaluate how effective your sales people are, and how well operations align with how a customer wants to be served. Spend time noticing and working on strategic, but not urgent issues. My hope is that the concept of Customer Aligned Selling will sink in, take root, and lead you to take action. If all you do is read this book, then you have not truly served your customer.

Read this book with the idea of transformation, not just a transaction. Transactional reading is giving yourself a check mark that you have read the book without making any changes. I have read *Achieve Sales Excellence* by Howard Stevens seventeen times and *Customer Centric Selling* by Michael Bosworth six times. Every time I read those books, I learned and applied something new. To change behavior, one must first change belief. My goal is to change your belief about how you sell and view your customers. Without a change in belief, no lasting improvement will happen. If you are a sales leader or business owner, you must model what you are teaching to your sales reps and customers.

I will use the terms "buyer" and "customer" interchangeably. Many have repeat customers, so every time the customer needs more of what you offer, they are a buyer.

I encourage you to reach out to me to discuss ways you can begin to implement Customer Aligned Selling™. I have begun with short workshops to introduce the concept and then moved elaborate in-house training and coaching. Each company begins at their pace.

Bill Hart
bill@billhartbizgrowth.com

# Chapter 1

# Sales - The Final Frontier

Sales Excellence is the final frontier for executives to gain a competitive advantage. Business leaders have spent the last 30 or so years focusing on building a better product, offering a better solution, and reducing price. Most companies are now competitively equal on those fronts. Sales excellence is truly adding continual value and serving the customer the way they want to be treated. Sound familiar? The final frontier of sales is the challenge of implementing the Platinum Rule: "Treat other people the way they want to be treated." In sales, that means, "Treat you customers the way they want you to treat them."

## Are your sales in good health?

Most people get an annual health checkup, but only few organizations get an annual sales checkup by a third party. Many CEOs attribute poor sales to the economy or increased pricing competition. From my observations, even if the economy improves, many organizations' sales do not. The economy is not the only issue. Outdated sales strategies and processes are causing such sales problems as alienated or frustrated buyers, delayed or canceled purchases, or outright rejection of the sales rep. Today's successful sales organizations *focus on the customer's needs, desired outcomes and how the customer makes a buying decision,* not on how the vendor wants to sell. All sales strategy and processes should be targeted to this fundamental change! That fundamental change is what this book is about.

## Developing an effective organization that lives and breathes true Customer Aligned Selling is the final frontier for most executives.

The Old Way Doesn't Work

**Are you basing your sales strategy on what worked in the past?** As Marshall Goldsmith said, "What got you here won't get you there."

The sales strategies and processes that previously worked for sales organizations are failing. Many sales leaders and CEOs, think that what worked in the past will work now and in the future. Unfortunately, that is not the case. Times have changed, and so have people's preferences. Everyone is inundated with advertising, social media, and other distractions. The 21$^{st}$ century buyer has rejected the process of being "sold to." Because of this fact, most sales organizations need a sales "physical" or assessment to determine if their strategy and processes align with the way customers want to buy.

The good news is that people still like to buy! Customers want to do business with companies who understand their business and can help them solve a problem, satisfy a need, achieve a goal, improve effectiveness, save time, and reduce expenses. They do not want simply to be sold some product or service to meet some sales rep's quota. Think about how you like to buy. If you were the customer, would you buy from some of your sales reps? go to www.billhartbizgrowth.com/salesassessment.

Impact of the Internet

In the past fifteen years, there has been a fundamental shift in the way buyers purchase. Much of the buying process has been automated.

Information Technology (IT) now plays a major role in everything from manufacturing to customer service. IT has eliminated many of the functions that a sales rep used to perform. The identification of a need, product research, and initial vendor selection can be all done without ever talking to a sales rep. With the Internet, customers do most the technical research online. They can shop for suppliers, and even compare companies via blogs, online ratings, and testimonials social media.

Before the Internet, the role of the sales rep was to educate a prospect through a presentation. If the presentation generated interest, the sales rep would qualify the prospect and then focus on closing the sale. The buyer welcomed cold calls and product presentations since that was the only to keep up with the latest developments in the market. From the seller's perspective, *everything about the sales process was related to creating a need, giving an opinion of how their product or service will meet the prospect's need, and then close the deal.* The old way of selling has very little effectiveness; due to the Internet and cultural shifts, people and the buying process have changed.

## Cold calling is no longer accepted.

The buyer can now get much of the technical details and even compare products and offerings down to the smallest of technical levels. Buyers can get pricing and other comparisons online. In many sales situations, the Internet has virtually eliminated the need for a sales rep during the first stage of the buying process, mapping the need to a particular solution. The very complex sale still requires a lot of technical discovery, but the buyer is very educated and most likely has already done a substantial amount of preliminary work. According to many sources from International Data Corporation (IDC) to Harvard Business School, anywhere from 50 - 70% of a decision to buy a product is made from Internet research without ever talking to a sales rep. Of course, the more complex and technical the sale, the less able the buyer is to decide from online research. But the buyer will do their research on the company, the reputation, and even the integrity of the individual sales rep. Social media can have a huge impact on a customer's selection of a company. For instance, LinkedIn is a great place to check on a sales rep's reputation and credibility. [1] Facebook can give clues to a sales rep's, or even a buyer's, personality and ethics. A seller's Tweets can reveal what they deem important.

Not only is the customer empowered, but now the sales rep is wise to make a call with knowledge about the company, its buying practices, departmental structure, and even the prospect's reputation. Hoovers, Manta, Data.com, and other websites and blogs are rich sources of such information. The rep should not be doing basic discovery of the prospective company's business, product lines, industry issues or other general business knowledge during the sales call. With the Internet, the rep should do that before the sales call. LinkedIn can provide valuable information as to the prospect's job history, who they know, and any key experiences to which the seller can relate. Facebook can tell you key things about their friends, family, or hobbies.

In fact, buyers expect that the rep has done his or her preliminary call preparation before the first sales call. The buyer does not tolerate such a waste of time from a rep who asks for information that can be found on the web. This relates to not only business but also personal information. [2]

## Do the basic customer discovery before the sales call.

---

[1] One thing to check on LinkedIn is how often a sales rep has changed jobs. That can tell their effectiveness in selling.

[2] Knowing personal information beforehand gives the sales rep specific topics to bring up versus just "fishing" for topics by looking at pictures or personal items in the prospect's office.

No More Cold Calls

In the majority of business to business sales (B2B), cold calling is either dead or breathing its last! Because of the Internet, very few buyers are tolerant of cold calls. I define a cold call from the customer's perspective: "I don't know who you are or why you are calling. I don't know if you offer any value. You are therefore a risk and will probably waste my time." To most buyers, a cold call is a waste of their time. The biggest challenge with a cold call is that the sales rep is calling a prospect with no reference that he or she can deliver value to the buyer. In other words, there is no trust in the relationship. From the prospect's perspective, by accepting the appointment, he or she is immediately at risk of wasting valuable time.

**Cold calls present risk, and beginning a relationship based upon risk is not a good way to start.**

Cold calls were accepted in the past because buyers were educated on new products and offerings through the sales rep. The buyer allowed for cold calls because there was no other way to be introduced to new or innovative solutions. With user groups, online executive forums, specific industry buyer groups, and search engines, the buyer does not need the rep to learn about a product or service. The customer can research his needs and find potential solutions without a sales rep. When a sales rep does make a call, a buyer can quickly validate the facts and learn whether the sales rep is blowing smoke or telling the truth.

With the great increases in personal productivity, people are expected to do more with less. So, buyers are busy doing their jobs, not listening to cold calling sales reps that have little to no specific knowledge of the buyer's true needs. In today's world, everyone has been conditioned to say "no" to cold calls. People are tired of being called at home and at work, hence the existence of the national Do Not Call Registry. Cold calling is DEAD for B2B selling! So, if you are an executive encouraging cold calling, STOP! You are creating problems for your sales reps and for potential customers. Teach your reps to make warm calls and get referrals. This may take longer, but the relationship will commence in the right manner, and not with assumptions of risk. A warm call is where the buyer knows who you are and why you are calling.

I hear from many "seasoned reps" that they have trouble selling to millennials. They complain that all the millennial buyer wants is the price. They claim that millennials don't value relationship selling. This seasoned sales rep's main methodology of selling has been on getting to know the person first, i.e. building relationship from a social perspective. This type of rep's sales call focused on talking a lot and learning about the buyer's personal life versus the buyer's business needs. The assumption was, "If the buyer likes me, then he will do business with me." Since millennials know they can get the information they need from the Internet, they are not tolerant of a sales rep who is basing winning the deal on likability. The millennial buyer may see the "seasoned "sales rep as just wasting their time. They may see no differential in product or solution offerings. Millennials are rejecting sellers who are selling from their comfort zone and buying preferences versus adapting to the millennials' buying preferences.

Lastly, buyers of today are not like the buyers of old. Many are professionally trained, are far more experienced, and have a greater level of expertise. The buyer is more technical and has, at their fingertips, access to most of the technical or supportive advice they need.

IT Plays a Major Role

Every business has streamlined its operational process through the use of Information Technology (IT). From Walmart to Mercedes, companies have built their entire supply chain around IT. Buyers today want suppliers who can add value. Customers want a supplier to have a systematic approach to meeting their needs. IT has changed much of the sales role internally from the seller's perspective: CRM, web-portals, email to the iPad. From the customer's perspective, IT's role is integration, fewer suppliers, tighter budgets, just-in-time delivery, etc. The results demonstrate that sales, as an area of business, is changing in three interrelated aspects: from a function to a process, from an isolated activity to an integrated one, and from an operational function to a strategic one. Senior level executives need to be involved in all aspects of the sales process from strategy, planning, compensation, and even to sales training (more on that reasoning later).

<u>Competence – Not Price, Product, or Offering</u>

## "Bring value!" cries the customer.

The buyer of today wants value and results starting with the first sales call. As mentioned, the sales process has changed. The buyer sees a "traditional" type of sales call where the sales rep leads a fact-finding interview (information that could be obtained via the web), or a presentation on the sales rep's company as a waste of time! The buyer of the 21st Century requires a sales rep to lead with the value he or she can bring.[3] Then the buyer will allow time for building rapport and working toward developing a credible solution. This is why a strong referral works so well, when the referral source tells your prospect that you have something of value to offer.

Summarizing interviews with over 80,000 customers and 7,500 sales reps over fourteen years of research, Howard Stevens, CEO of Chally Assessments, demonstrates this point by explaining what is important to buyers in their decision of choosing a vendor in his book, *Achieve Sales Excellence.* The sales rep's competence and the value he or she brings during the complete sales process represent 39% of the buyer's decision. Offering a total solution represents only 22% of the buyer's decision. Having a quality offering represents 21% of the decision, and

---

[3] The challenge with millennials is what they value is not based upon relationship thus the seasoned rep must have a new value-based approach. This requires creativity and work.

price only influences the decision to buy by 18%. Unfortunately, most organizations spend the major portion of sales effort and money on the latter three points. Do you see a problem with this approach? Quality, solution, and competitive pricing are now de-facto requirements of doing business; without those, a company can't even get in the door. For the past 30 years CEOs' efforts have been on quality, total solution, and price.

The final frontier is sales competence – training and managing your sales force and designing your sales operations to serve the customer the way they want to be served throughout the entire relationship.

# The Customer Aligned Selling Process in Seven Steps

Customer Aligned Selling Process

Cog 1. This first stage is about preparation, developing a value proposition that has substantiated value, prospecting, and setting appointments. This is where the buyer must believe there is value to have a conversation. The value proposition must relate to the buyer's problems, needs, or goals.

Cog 2. During the first meeting, engage in meaningful conversation with the focus on the buyer(s) and their problems, goals, and needs. This is where the value proposition is specifically aligned and elaborated on using examples from the buyer's own issues.

Cog 3. Discuss solutions using stories and examples relating the solution (product or service) to how the buyer would use it in their organization. Identify the buyer's decision criteria and where they are in their buying process – Solution Development, Evaluation or Commitment (see Chapter 13).

Cog 4. The sales rep and the buyer craft a solution that will meet their decision criteria and fits within their expectations. This requires the sales rep to specifically discuss how the buyer will use the product or service and how success will be measured.

Cog 5. The risk of not getting the desired outcome is top of the buyer's mind before they buy. The sales rep works to ensure risk is reduced, negotiates on buyer specifics terms, and gets buyer commitment.

Cog 6. This stage is where the delivery of the solution takes place. This is where operations are aligned with delivering what sales has negotiated. The delivery of the product or service is oriented to the customer and is in alignment with the customer expectations.

Cog 7. The customer receives their desired outcome. If this is a product or service that is repeatable, then the process may start over again from the beginning or may engage with the latter cogs. The key is that the sales rep is in alignment with the customer's buying process.

Effective, open-ended questions are the lubricant or oil that enables to cogs to move freely.

The remainder of this book will cover the specifics of each phase/cog, and specific guidelines and exercises to move through each phase.

# Chapter 2

# Selling is a Beauty Contest, Not a Race

Remember, "Selling is a beauty contest, not a race." To win a beauty contest, you must know what the judges are expecting and the criteria from which they will judge. So, slow down and remember that your prospect or customer has the gold and makes the rules. Their rule is the Platinum Rule. If you apply these principles in this book, you will win the beauty contest and be a top performer. It won't be easy, but these principles will make you more money.

Let's look at how a contestant engages in a beauty contest. First, the contestant will want to know the rules of the contest – what is being judged such as looks, poise, posture, hair, evening gown, etc. Secondly, the contestant wants to know who the judges are; who will make the decision. They don't just want to know who the judges are, but also want to know if the judges have ever judged another beauty contest, and if so, what did they judge, when, and how did they score the contestants? Past decisions of judging will always affect the present contest either positively or negatively. The most competitive contestant will also want to know, if possible, does the judge favor one particular type of contestant over another? Does the judge have a preference in colors? What their view is on certain societal issues? If the contestant doesn't know these issues, then they don't know how best to answer questions to the judge's liking. The contestant wants to know everything they can about the judges, their decision criteria, and who possibly might be influencing them.

Identifying the judge's criteria does not mean that the contestant is not authentically themselves. They present themselves to the best of their ability, not faking anything, but in a manner that is most favorable to the judges. I am not proposing the old sales adage, "Fake it until you make it." Authenticity is of who you truly are is key in all situations.

When I gave this example of a beauty contest to Robert Raiford, Senior Vice President at Southland International Trucks in Birmingham, AL, he laughed and said that he had been a judge in a beauty contest three years ago. Robert is progressive in his politics and asked a contestant a question related to a woman being president. The contestant gave a very traditional, very culturally southern answer, much to Robert's distaste. If she had known his views or even done a little home work on the organizations he participates in and what boards he is on all of which is public information, she might have had more knowledge of the type of answer he might favor.

One of my client's managers is an advisor to the Miss Alabama Pageant. She says that she must coach guest judges on how to judge.

First, these judges are typically over age 50, so they will probably have a certain bias to the way pageants were done in the past, even though many rules have changed and what is evaluated has progressed. She says, "If I don't teach them how to judge a pageant in 2016, all the contestants that win will look like they came from 1980s or 1990s." Without proper education, many judges would use the wrong judging criteria.

Since the contest is not a race, the contestant takes her time as she demonstrates her best attributes. You don't see her running to get to the end of the stage, spinning around a few times, and saying, "Pick me!" Too many sales people focus on closing the deal and therefore make the sales process a race to see how fast they can get the sale closed.

The same judging issues that relate to a beauty contest relate to selling and understanding your buyer. As sales rep, you must understand their buying criteria, past and present, for without it you are just hoping you will make the sale. Hope is a very poor sales strategy. Many times, a sales rep may need to educate or re-educate a buyer on how to make the right decision. Many sales are left "dead in the water" for the buyer did not know how to decide. They buyer had never made this type of decision before so they did not know how to evaluate the seller's offering.

I am currently working with a bathroom remodeling company. The first thing I did was to assess their sales process, which I learned did not include ascertaining whether the buyer had ever remodeled a bathroom and how successful the experience was. They did not ask questions as to what their buying criteria was in the past or what it will be for this decision, so the sales rep does not know what the buyer's experience or expectations are for his sales call. Thus, there was no place in the sales process to pause and spend time educating the buyer on how to make a decision, i.e. define what is good buying criteria for remodeling a bathroom. The sales process just assumed that people knew what they wanted or that they could be persuaded to buy what the sales rep offered through a features and benefits presentation.

Since people rarely have any experience in remodeling a bathroom, they don't know what criteria to use to decide to buy. What happens is the sales reps present their solution, saying "Our solution is by far superior to traditional bathroom remodeling," but many buyers do not know how to distinguish which is the best choice or why moving ahead with the purchase is a win for them. The buyer says, "Let me think about it" and does nothing.

My focus on improving their sales process is two-fold: 1) determine the prospect's previous remodeling experience, if any and 2) incorporate teaching the buyer how to make a decision very early in the sales process. So, when the presentation is made, the buyer understands and can make a value judgement on what is offered versus using a traditional contractor installing tile.

Here is some of the dialogue that should take place:

"Hi, Mrs. Homeowner, I am Bill with the Bath Remodeling Company. To make sure we have a successful meeting today and I don't waste your time, before I begin talking about your needs and desires, may I ask you a few questions?

The first question is related to their expectations: "What do you want to accomplish today with me being in your home?"

"Have you ever remodeled a bathroom before?"

If so, "Please share your experience with me – was it positive or negative? What were the reasons you made those choices?"

If not, "May I share with you some of the key criteria that most homeowners use in designing a bathroom and choosing a remodeler?"

"The first issue we can discuss is materials…" The sales rep would educate the homeowner on key issues of remodeling a bathroom. As they go investigate the current bathroom, the sales rep could continue the education process.

Assessment

1. Do I treat my sales process as a race with my focus being to get the client to buy?
2. Is getting deals closed at the top of my mind because I am motivated by my quota?

# Chapter 3

# The Traditional Rep VS. the Customer Aligned™ Rep

<u>The Sales Call – Comparing the Old Way with the New</u>

I have been sharing the steps to develop a Customer Aligned sales process. This chapter is where we put it all together comparing the old with the new. Ask yourself, "Which person does my sales methodology most resemble?"

Below is a chart[4] that compares the traditional way of selling with a customer aligned approach. The old perspective is from the seller's point of view. The Customer Aligned Selling approach is one with the customer/ buyer's viewpoint in mind.

With the old way of selling, the sales rep's main objective is to create a transaction, to get the customer to buy. "I need to make my quota; please buy from me." The new way is focused on identifying if the customer truly has a need, problem, or goal, then helping them achieve their desired outcome. As Stephen Covey says, "Begin with the end in mind." By beginning the discussion with the customer's end in mind, the sales rep gains credibility, builds trust, and has an opportunity to add value at every step of the process.

---

[4] Modified chart from Customer Centric Selling by Michael T. Bosworth and John R. Holland.

| The Old Way | Customer Aligned Selling™ |
|---|---|
| Make presentations | Have a Situational Discussion |
| Offer opinions | Ask relevant questions |
| Relationship focused | Solutions focused |
| Gravitate toward users | Target business people |
| Rely on product | Relate product usage |
| Attempt to sell by convincing, persuading, handling objections, overcoming resistance | Empower the Buyer |
| Reps need to be managed | Reps manage their managers |

Let's say there is a sales rep named Barbara. In the old, or traditional model of selling, Barbara is taught by her company to make a presentation on what they sell. To ensure that the presentation is consistent among all sales reps, the marketing department develops a features and benefits analysis, and then creates a presentation that all reps should learn. So, Barbara learns a PowerPoint presentation, and the marketing department or the sales manager trains Barbara on how these features and benefits will solve the customer's problems. Sound familiar?

Armed with a fancy presentation, some slick brochures, and maybe some product samples, Barbara hits the street. She knows that people do business with people they like, so she spends some time trying to build rapport. Once Barbara feels like enough rapport is built, she seeks the opportunity to make a presentation showing features and benefits. Barbara may even probe for problems that she can relate to the features and benefits. When a problem, need, or goal is uncovered, Barbara says, "You know what will work for you..." and proceeds to tell the buyer how her company's products or services can solve that need. She is now giving her opinion. That opinion is typically related to how the product or service will magically solve the buyer's problems. At this point, she is talking, and not discussing. In the prospect's mind, Barbara is being a little audacious or arrogant, even if she does not intend to be, by telling the buyer how she or her company will solve the buyer's problems.

With this type of training and presentation, a rep like Barbara typically gets delegated down to the level in the organization that is interested in features. For a copier salesperson, the features are feeds, speed, and multi-functions, and the rep is delegated to the office manager. A drug rep might open with, "How many samples do you need?" and they are delegated to the nurse. When software company reps present bells and whistles, functions, and interconnections to other software talking database interconnectivity, they are delegated to a midlevel manager in IT. When I sell my sales training, if I focus on the cost of the training and the venue, I generally get delegated to the sales manager, the sales event coordinator, or even the HR director.

Once Barbara is delegated to a certain level in which she and the user are comfortable, talking features, benefits, etc., she then focuses on building and establishing a good relationship. She will say, "Hey, buyer, let's go play golf or have lunch." She is thinking this mid-level manager is the key person; he is the one who decides what to purchase. Barbara's goal of the time spent with the buyer is to build relationship. Since people do business with those they like, she tries to get the buyer to be her "buddy." With the relationship as the focus of Barbara's efforts, she relies on the product's/service's features/benefits to be the main sales driver.

In general, during this sales effort or even after a sale, the way a traditional sales rep typically handles a problem is to focus on the relationship, and not how to solve the problem. The rep relies on rapport and friendship to keep the business, not on his or her ability to solve the problem.

Since Barbara has been taught to create a transaction, all her effort is focused on getting to the close. If there are delays or objections, she attempts to close by convincing, persuading, handling objections, and overcoming resistance. If that does not work, the next tactic is to drop price. Barbara's efforts are to manipulate the buyer into buying. Barbara's focus is on meeting her quota, getting her commission, or keeping the manager of her back.

Reps like Barbara must be managed. Sales managers spend most of their day overseeing these types of activities. Sales managers end up picking up the dropped pieces or solving problems that the typical rep cannot handle. Sales managers spend much time filling out reports and managing reps' activity. Without realizing it, the sales managers are perpetuating the rep's poor sales behavior. By helping the rep manage the crisis they created, the sales manager is teaching the rep that problem-solving and being proactive is not a required sales skill.

This type of selling has a very steep declining return. The more buyers experience the customer aligned sales rep, the quicker they will jettison the old-style rep. For instance, when a Customer Aligned trained rep calls on Barbara's client and treats them with a Customer Aligned Sales approach, the client is refreshed and engages the rep in a true discussion. Barbara tries to reach the buyer, but they will not answer Barbara's emails or voice mails. She does not know it, but Barbara is about to lose a prospect or a client.

Customer Aligned Selling™

Customer Aligned Sales reps begin every sales call with the goal of creating value during every interaction with the prospect or customer. Customer Aligned reps understand what the new sales solution is: value = trust. If their focus is on adding value to the prospect/customer during every interaction, the prospect will trust them. Trust leads to true and loyal relationships. These types of relationships lead to repeat business.

How does the Customer Aligned rep create value? Let's use another fictitious sales rep named Jim. First, Jim is aware that cold calling is dead and business people want to know who you are and why you are calling before the initial introduction. The value Jim brings with that knowledge is not wasting the buyer's time with an unsolicited call. Jim uses referrals[5] or letters of introduction. Once Jim has the appointment, he prepares thoroughly by gaining knowledge about the company, the industry, and the person he is calling on through Google and LinkedIn.

During the meeting, Jim engages the prospect in a discussion related to their specific situation. He does not talk about his product or services, but engages the prospect in terms of the market and what is happening at the prospect's company. Through a situational discussion, Jim is probing for needs, goals, and problems. He is asking intelligent and relevant questions. Jim knows that engaging the prospect and focusing on value through relevant questions is the fastest way to build rapport. Jim speaks the language of the prospect, remembering that if he gets too technical with upper level executives, he will get delegated down. If it is a CFO, Jim talks about the cost of capital, industry verses company rate of return, or margins. If it is a plant manager, Jim may talk about up-time or maintenance issues and how they relate to serving the customer. Jim has targeted decision-makers, not users, for his sales calls. Users can talk about features and benefits but they cannot make buying decisions.

One of Jim's key skills is that he asks four to six questions related to an issue. Once he has discovered a problem, goal, or need, he digs deeper. He does not assume he knows what the core issue behind the goal, problem, or need is. He asks deeper questions, such as, "When you solve that problem, what does that do for you and the company?" Jim is seeking to understand personal motives and corporate directions. He may even ask a follow-up question like, "When that problem is solved, who is most positively affected?", "How does solving this problem affect annual goals and even three-year goals?" or, "How does this affect you personally, making your job more enjoyable or your team more effective?" Jim is trying to get to the core or root of the issue. Some sales

---

[5] LinkedIn can play a major role in getting referrals.

professionals have labeled that core issue as the Prime Buying Motive – business and personal. The prime buying motive is what will drive the intellectual and emotional decision to buy.

When it is appropriate to discuss Jim's offerings, he discusses them in terms of outcomes. He *shares* the outcomes his company's products or services have helped deliver with other customers. Jim relates product or service usage to possible solutions and then waits for the decision maker to tell him that a particular product or service would also work in their environment. A key point in this scenario is that Jim does not **tell** the buyer what will work, but shares or relates how others have used his product or service and the outcomes they have achieved. He then asks the prospect, based upon similar usage, if they expect to see the same outcome. Jim knows that the he does not have a solution until the buyer agrees that Jim's offerings could work at the buyer's company. By sharing potential solutions, delivering a specific outcome, and getting the buyer to agree, Jim is not just offering his opinion, as most sales reps do. He is leading the buyer to a discovery of how to solve a problem or satisfy a need. He knows that he does not have a solution until the buyer tells him so!

After the meeting, Jim sends a summary covering the topics, gaps that need addressing, potential solutions, and agreed upon next steps. After two weeks, as promised, Jim connects the CFO to another CFO at one of his clients who have similar issues and were interested in meeting. During the buying process, Jim stays in communication with his prospect and works proactively to answer questions, obtain the right resources, and reduce the CFO's risk of moving forward with his solution. Jim's goal is empowering the customer to achieve their desired results. Another benefit is knowing that he will benefit financially and create a loyal customer. Jim applies the 7 Rules of the Customer (see Chapter 8 for details) to keep and grow the business.

Jim is a Sales Manager's dream. He requires little management, and from an internal perspective, he manages his manager through the sales and delivery process. Jim effectively represents his customer to his manager and directs him with regard to how he can use his management power to get things done to best serve the customer. Since Jim has his manager's trust, his manager responds to unique requests and urgent issues in a welcome manner.

## 7 Rules of the Customer

1. You must be personally accountable for our results.
2. You must understand our business.
3. You must be on our side.
4. You must bring us applications, not just products.
5. You must be easily accessible.
6. You must solve our problems.
7. You must be innovative in responding to our needs.

Assessment

- Is the main focus of our sales process to close the deal?
- Do I begin my meetings talking about our company versus learning about their specific situations?
- How much preparation work do I do before a meeting? ____ minutes/hours?
- Is building relationship (likeability) my main methodology for creating new business?
- Do I spend a lot of time talking versus asking probing questions?
- Do I rely on the product or solution and our company's reputation to close the business?
- Do I begin with a presentation?
- Do I use price ("You'll get a great deal.") as the main motivator or determinant of why they buy?
- Do I use our company's service ("We offer quality.") as the main reason to buy?
- Do I use "closing techniques," like manipulation and handling objections?

# Chapter 4

# Customer Reasons and Motives

There are two forces that drive a customer's buying decision: business reasons and personal motives. A successful sale depends on your ability to accurately identify the reason your customer has for buying and what he's looking for in a vendor. If you fall short in either area, you are likely to lose the sale.

To understand these forces and how they relate to each other, it helps to imagine a business as a bicycle[1]. On a bicycle, the rear wheel is where the force that propels the bike forward is applied. The front wheel is the one that controls the bike's direction.

In sales, your customer is a bike rider, and the wheels of his bike represent the reasons and motives behind his buying decision. The rear wheel is the business reasons that drive your customer to buy, i.e. his needs or desired outcome. The front wheel is the factor that determines the direction in which he will go - whether he buys from you or from someone else – and is usually determined by personal motives.

For sales success, it is critical to realize that the two cannot be separated. The sales rep who best understands and addresses both the business reasons and personal motives will be the one who wins. The sales rep who fails to understand either wheel will find his customer steering in another direction.

# Two Buying Reasons

**Driving Force**     **Direction**

## Business Drivers - Revenue, Expenses, and Risk

There are three business drivers behind most buying decisions: revenue, expenses, and risk. The goal of all businesses is to increase profits, survive, and grow. Profits are affected by these three things, and thus customers buy your product or services for three primary and interrelated reasons.

## Increase or Protect Revenue

Business leaders seek to *increase* revenue by hiring a marketing firm to improve their brand or image in the market place. They may purchase a product or service to improve sales productivity such as a CRM, a leads database, or sales training. They hire more sales reps or expand into new territories to increase revenue. New products or offerings are launched into the market place to increase revenue.

Leaders often *protect* revenue by buying their competition. Microsoft is one company who has done this several times to eliminate a superior software product; Microsoft buys the company and then either shelves the technology or integrates it into their own offerings. Companies will sell at a loss or even open non-productive territories to keep the competition from establishing a foothold. Non-compete contracts are required by employees to protect revenue.

Reduce or Control Expenses

Reducing expenses goes directly to the bottom line, increases profits, and may also allow funds to be redirected toward generating revenue. Companies may reduce expenses by changing health insurance plans, consolidating suppliers, or hiring consultants to improve productivity with fixed resources. Companies will also focus on keeping expenses flat, i.e. controlling expenses, by seeking greater efficiencies in operations and leveraging existing resources to a greater extent. Controlling expenses can enable a company to grow without increasing overhead.

I had a client whose sales were down, making the operational overhead expenses as a percentage of sales higher than he wanted, so he laid off several operations people to reduce their total overhead. When the Affordable Care Act hit, I know of several companies that totally restructured their healthcare plans, switching to new insurance companies with the goal of keeping health insurance expenses flat or controlling the growth of that expense.

Risk

Managing or offsetting risk is critical for business continuity. Companies take great care in putting measures in place to ensure they can continue to operate after a disaster or crisis disrupts business. Ensuring the protection of company data, intellectual or physical property, safety, the wellbeing of employees, and other key issues are all about mitigating risk, which is closely tied to reasons 1 and 2.

Offsite back up for data, or moving the data to the "cloud," is a common practice for reducing risk. Implementing wellness plans for employees encourages better health, which reduces the sick days and downtime. Safety programs reduce employee injuries, which affect productivity and increase expenses. Errors and Omissions, liability, fire and key man life insurance protects business continuity. Fences and locks on doors protect physical property from damage. All these are methods used to reduce risk, thereby protecting revenue and avoiding the expenses associated with these types of loss.

## Determine the buying reason related to revenue, expenses, and risk.

Since increasing or protecting revenue, reducing or controlling expenses, and reducing risk are the foundation of all buying decisions, your conversations should always be targeted to impacting these three areas. Buyers are communicating with you because they desire to achieve an outcome; therefore, all sales calls should be made with the goal of understanding the desired outcome and how it impacts your customer's business drivers.

Here is a simple exercise you or your sales team can do to make sure you address these concerns. For each of your products/services, answer the three questions below and prepare examples or illustrative stories around each.

1. How do my products/services help increase or protect revenue?
2. How do my products/services reduce or control expenses?
3. How do my products/services reduce risk to:
   o People
   o Data
   o Business Continuity
   o Finances

If you are a sales manager, a great way to do this with your team is to assign a product or service to each of your sales reps and have them complete the exercise. Then have a meeting where each person presents his/her responses and have group discussion to share ideas on how to refine and improve the talking points for that particular product/service.

Too many sales reps present features and benefits without ever understanding if or how their product or service impacts the customer in these areas. Those who identify needs, problems, and/or goals and work on tying their products and services to the buyer's desired outcome are in much better position to earn the sale. And they typically do.

<u>Personal Motives</u>

Personal motives are driven by your customer's core desires and values. There are four main categories of personal motives: power, approval, comfort, and security.

There are many subcategories to each of these, and paying attention to your customer's comments will help you figure out what his exact motives are. Here are some of the most common personal motives and the categories into which they fall:

**POWER**

- Significance; feeling part of a higher purpose
- Sees the big picture
- Need to win
- Seeking more control (this is typically to minimize risk or control others)
- Revenge or to get even
- Enjoys taking risk
- Fun, Innovation
- Career advancement

## APPROVAL

- Recognition from others, the need to hear "well done"
- Approval by a superior or a peer, or even employees
- Desire to be a hero
- Affiliation- being accepted by a group
- Team buy-in
- Respect by others
- Fun, Innovation

## COMFORT

- Pursuing peace, reducing chaos or stress
- To love or care for another
- To be loved by another
- Seeking rest
- Religious beliefs or values
- Significance; feeling part of a higher purpose
- Aesthetics, beauty

## SECURITY

- Fear – avoidance of a negative outcome
- Minimize personal risk
- Revenge or to get even
- Religious beliefs or values

Notice that some of these fall into more than one category. You'll need to ask the right kind of question to figure out what's really behind what your customer is saying. To address personal motives, you first must figure out what they are. This is a simple, two-step process.

First, listen for keywords in your customer's comments. Your customer will tell you his reasons; you only have to listen for hints in what he says. For instance, if a person says, "My team/boss/co-workers will really love this," that could be a hint that approval is one of his motives. If someone says, "We are trying to reduce complexity in our expense process," that is a hint toward comfort (less stress).

But since some of the keywords you'll be listening for fall into more than one category you'll need to ask the right questions to figure out where your customer is coming from.

Next, follow up with "what" and "how" questions, not "why". When you hear clues to personal buying motives, ask your follow-up questions without using the word "why." It insinuates motive, and your customer may not be as forthcoming as you'd like.

"How" and "what" questions are more effective in getting a person to reveal his or her why. Ask questions like, "When (the hint they just gave you) happens, what will it do for you?" or, "What will that give you?" Then follow up with, "And how is that important?" Their answer will give you more concrete evidence of their personal buying motive.

Remember that to succeed in sales, it is critical to realize that your customer's personal motives cannot be separated from his business reasons for buying. The bicycle can't move forward without both wheels. Failing to understand or disregarding either wheel will cause your customer to steer in another sales rep's direction. Careful listening and framing of your follow-up questions can make you the rep who wins.

For example, I once spent 9 months on retainer with a local utility teaching Customer Aligned Selling™ to the sales/marketing department. The business driver was to increase the number of customers, revenue, and to spread overhead over the customer base (a utility is regulated in terms of expenses and overhead based upon the number of customers). The personal motive of the senior vice president was that he liked innovation, so the big-picture approach of how I addressed the sales problem and the analytical approach of psychological analysis I brought to the training and transformation process appealed to him. And lastly, he wanted to see his team have buy-in.

In working with a physical therapy company, the business goal was to double referrals, but the personal motive was respect for her team; therefore, the owner's staff must like me and buy into what I was teaching. I had to be interviewed by several staff members to get their buy-in before I was hired. They later told me that the reason the other consultant was not hired was that the staff did not like him. The owner's personal values also played a key role in who she hired; she wanted someone with the same religious values as she had.

A regional oil lubricants supplier wanted to increase sales by 10% and reduce overhead per sale by 25%, so revenue and expenses were the business drivers. The personal motives were based upon their learning styles, the logic behind the material, and ability to get team buy-in. They judged me from a very analytical standpoint and event sent several people to a class I teach to "test" his people's buy-in and see if I was presenting data and facts versus anecdotal stories before he hired me for in-house training.

## Assessment

1. On a percentage basis, how often do you have the business criteria fully identified before you make a product or service presentation?
2. How often do you know their personal motives?
3. Evaluate your 4 last sales and identify the business reasons and the personal reasons.

## Exercise

Answer these questions for all your products and services and give examples or develop stories around each scenario. An easy way to do this is to assign a product or service to each one of your sales reps and have them complete the exercise. Then, have a meeting where each person presents the information and have discussion.

1. How my products/services help increase or protect revenue?
2. How my products/services reduce or control expenses?
3. How my products/services reduce risk:

    1. People
    2. Data
    3. Business Continuity
    4. Financial

# Chapter 5

## Golden Rules and Love Languages = Platinum

In business, there are two Golden Rules you must abide by to be successful. The first is the Biblical Golden Rule: "Do unto others as you would have them do unto you." The second is the business Golden Rule: "He who has the gold makes the rules."

These rules clearly emphasize that successful companies understand the customer's perspective in the sales and delivery of product or services. For many companies, their entire sales process is designed from their perspective, what their needs are, and what they want to sell. Not only are sales processes developed introspectively, but many times, the operations side of the business is functioning without customer input. Operations are doing things the way they have always done them, unless demanded by a client to do something unique.

Relating to operations, that is Cog 6 in the Customer Aligned Selling diagram where operational alignment is key to helping the client/customer achieve their desired outcomes.

From the customer's perspective, the Golden Rules say, "Respect me and understand that if you want my gold, you must abide by my rules."

Another way to explain seeing your customer from their perspective is an example using relationships between people, especially in family or marriage. In his research of family and relationships, Dr. Gary Chapman documented that there are five ways of expressing and receiving love. He calls these the "five love languages," and most people have two that are dominant. They five love languages are:

1. Words of affirmation: speaking and hearing words that are affirming, encouraging, and positive.
2. Receiving a gift: because it says the other person thought of you and cared for you.
3. Quality time: giving and receiving a person's undivided attention.
4. Physical touch; nothing speaks more deeply than giving or receiving appropriate touch.
5. Acts of service: doing something that is unsolicited for someone out of love, not out of obligation.

*Go to www.5lovelanguages.com for a free assessment to determine your and your significant other's love languages*

People give love and expect to receive love in one or two of these ways. The challenge is when people's love languages do not align. For instance, if a husband's love language is acts of service and gift giving, the way he loves his wife is caring for her car and doing things around the house, such as laundry and dishes. He frequently buys her gifts running the gamut from little things to expensive items. There will be problems if his wife's love languages are quality time and words of affirmation. What she wants from her husband is his undivided attention and to hear him speak words that affirm her and their relationship. She would like to be recognized verbally and have him leave her love notes. No matter how much effort the husband puts into serving his wife and buying her gifts, she is not going to feel the love. No matter how much she affirms her husband and gives him undivided attention, he is not going to feel loved until she does things for him and buys him gifts. Unless love is expressed toward a person in one of the love languages they speak, they will not perceive it as love.

The **Platinum Rule** is a combination of the Golden Rules and love languages. The Platinum rule in sales is, "Sell to me the way I want to buy. Engage with me on my terms, seeking to understand my situation, preferences and criteria. Don't present the way you want to sell. Deliver services the way I want to experience them, not how you want to deliver them."

Most sales reps were taught to sell the features and benefits of a product or service and to tell the prospect how it will benefit them. In that manner of selling, the sales rep typically presents the product from his or her perspective and tells the client how it will benefit them instead of engaging in a discussion to identify the prospect's buying criteria and their desired outcomes. A sales process that focuses more on *telling* than asking in-depth, open-ended discovery questions is not adapting to the buyer's buying processes. It is very seller-centric. Many sales reps wonder why they don't get a second chance to meet with the buyer. The reason is that the seller was not applying the Platinum Rule. The rep should have been learning about the customer, their goals, problems, or needs, how they want to engage, and their desired outcomes before a presentation or proposal is ever made.

Here is an example of the Platinum Rule not being implemented in operations. When working with a local utility, the operations division, which installed the utilities connecting into new buildings and homes, had the same phone number residential and commercial customer support. That meant that contractors, home owners, and large manufacturers all had to call the same number and talk with someone in the call center. Contractors and large manufacturers wanted a separate line so they could talk with the right people quickly. The way the call center was operating, there was no way to treat commercial customers any different than residential customers. This system was designed from an internal perspective without ever asking their commercial customers how they could be better served by the call center. If the utility had approached their customers from the Platinum perspective and listened, they would have developed a different way to run the call center, creating separate lines and support staff to serve residential and commercial customers more efficiently.

Another example is a regional accounting firm that was working on how they tracked billing. Customers were complaining about being billed for time spent on things they did not see as adding value. The partner explained it as "gray time" when the accountant may be working on something related to the client, but not adding tangible value to the client. One example he gave was charging the client for a courier service when the client was less than a mile from their office. The internal billing process required accounting for all time throughout a day, but the customer saw that being charged for delivery was frivolous. The Platinum Rule was not applied.

When business leaders understand the Platinum Rule and apply it in the sales process, customers buy, and they buy often. As you read this book, I encourage you to further apply this concept internally with operations and externally with customers. Do to your customer as they would have you do to them. Understand their business from their perspective. Help the prospect buy, don't sell to them!

The true spirit of the Platinum Rule is just that: think of others first. In the Holy Bible, Jesus said the second greatest commandment was, "…to love your neighbor as yourself."[6] With that truth, your challenge or obligation as a sales leader or rep is to apply the Platinum Rule and treat your customers the way they want to be treated, according to their criteria of excellence.

The positive news on the story related to the local utility is that one-third of the operations staff were put under the control of the Business Development department, and a high-level operations executive was

---

[6] Mark 12:31 from the Holy Bible

transferred to that department to help coordinate operations, support sales efforts, and be focused on what the customer truly wants. I worked with the sales reps teaching and coaching on Customer Aligned Selling™. The result was that sales went up and customer's satisfaction improved.

Assessment

1. What are the core purposes of your sales call: to help yourself or to help the customer?
2. How much time do you spend preparing to understand a customer's issues from their perspective before and during the sales call?
3. Ask your customers if they feel your product and service delivery aligns with their goals and needs.

# Chapter 6

# The 21ˢᵗ Century Sales Equation

## Solution selling is the old equation

Solution selling became very popular in the late 1980s and 1990s and hit its peak following the best-selling book, *SPIN Selling* by Neil Rackham. The focus of solution selling was on engaging the prospect in a real problem-solving conversation and digging until you found the need. Then the sales rep's job was to demonstrate how his or her solution would best meet that need and provide the proper outcome. This was different from the old sales process of beginning with a presentation and hoping that the buyer saw relevance to their situation.

Solution selling is based on some assumptions about the prospect that are no longer valid. The first assumption is that the prospect is not very educated on the solutions available in the market place, therefore he will give the sales rep lots of discovery time to understand his business and identify a need or problem. The Internet erased that assumption. The prospect is now very educated on options in the market and expects the sales rep to understand their industry, common needs, and problems already. He is not willing to allow a lot of time for the rep to be interview him to learn about the company and identify problems or needs.

The second assumption is that there are significant differences in products and services in terms of solutions offered and quality of those solutions. Between the 1980s and early 2000, there were differences in quality of offerings. But due to a heavy investment in lean manufacturing, ISO 9000 processes, and Total Quality Management, in addition to the impact of social media telling the true story about a product or offering, companies today have developed offerings that do meet market demand and have solved most of quality issues. In the 21st century, if a company does not have a valid offering with the required quality, they can't stay in business, so the prospect knows that whoever he talks with will have a feasible solution that can work.

Take selling copiers as an example. From the 1970s-1990s, Xerox had a substantial competitive advantage on the quality, features, and functionality of copiers and printers. Using the solution selling approach, the sales rep just had to uncover the need a company was having due to an inferior copier or one that could not meet all their print management needs. Then he or she would present the Xerox solution as better, with more features and functionality, and/or quality, while validating the return on investment to win the deal. In 2016, all copiers/printers can do everything a Xerox can do with equal quality. Consequently, Xerox's sales strategy is now to focus on what value they can add in terms of services to win major deals.

Because all products and services claim to be equal or at least deliver what is promised, the buyer shifted from looking for the best solution to looking for the vendor/supplier providing the most value. That value starts with the sales rep delivering value from the first sales call.

Value = Trust is the 21st century sales equation. The responsibility of the sales rep is to focus on how they can add value from the very first sales call, knowing that value will cumulatively lead to building trust.

The 21st century customer demands value at every step of the relationship. The 21st Century sales rep, who demonstrates value at the beginning of the relationship, builds trust. Building trust is what advances the sales opportunity. Adding value is accomplished by:

1) Proper training of the sales rep to see the situation from the buyer's perspective.

2) Making the sales call with most of factual information already collected via the Internet or communicating with key players in the industry.

3) Having knowledge of key industry issues and specific business issues that affect the success of the prospect's company (the buyer does not have to educate the seller on their business or industry).

4) Being able to teach or educate the buyer on how to better run their business or department, or see situations from a new perspective (the Challenger sales concept7).

5) Asking relevant questions that lead to a viable solution positively impacting revenue, expenses, or risk.

The customer wants the sales rep to understand their industry and know their business and their industry's specific challenging issues. The rep builds value in the process of how he or she serves the customer. Today's successful sales organizations focus on the customer's needs and how they buy, not on how the vendor wants to sell. This is accomplished by creating a sales process that delivers value at each step of the customer's buying process. *All sales strategies and processes should be targeted to this fundamental change.* You can add value by speaking the customer's language, understanding their business issues, and relating how your product or service can solve their specific issues.

For example, using the 5 steps above:

1) The sales rep has been taught to relate the solution to how it impacts revenue, expenses, and risk. The rep can give specific examples, stories or metrics in how the offering can potentially impact company goals. The sales rep can speak the language of the buyer. If a CFO, then the rep can talk in terms of return on investment, cost of capital, or overhead expenses.

---

[7] The Challenger Sale: Taking Control of the Customer Conversation by Matthew Dixon and Brent Adamson

2) The sales rep has a strong knowledge of the company gained from annual reports, press announcements, or conversations with a supplier who sells to that company.

3) The sales rep has done research and/or talked with others in the industry to know the key market issues affecting that company and the industry as a whole. The sales rep may have talked with a banker who calls on that company or particular industry to glean more specific knowledge.

4) The rep is aware of specific areas that could be improved and has effectively helped other companies in this area. The rep has developed effective communication and educating skills to engage the prospect in a discussion without lecturing. The education happens in a conversational manner.

5) The rep has come prepared with relevant questions and has an agenda that is shared with the prospect. The questions asked are developed to lead into more detail and focus on problems and goals, not just general "get to know you" questions (see sample questions on the Client Worksheet in Chapter 15).

## All sales strategies should have focus on delivering value

In the book, *The Challenger Sale: Taking Control of the Customer Conversation*, Matthew Dixon and Brent Adamson emphasize that the most effective sales reps not only understand the business and industry, but are capable of educating their prospect on something they did not know. The sales rep is educating the buyer in the sales process, thus adding value. In this education process, the sales rep is collaborating with the buyer to craft the desired solution.

Customer Aligned Selling inspires buyers with new ideas, being innovative in how they bring value in helping achieve a goal. The focus is on a better future, and where necessary, pushing back against the status quo. The goal is to help the buyer see new possibilities, and even new ways of making a buying decision that will be to their benefit.

# The 21ˢᵗ Century Sales Equation is Value = Trust.

When you add value at every step, you build cumulative trust. It is hard for a competitor to compete, even with a lower price, when you have built cumulative trust.

## The Path to Value and Trust

B.F. Skinner's Ph.D. work in behavioral psychology, more specifically operant conditioning, identified the causes and effects of behavior, and how consequences of behavior determine future behaviors. Operant conditioning is a type of learning in which the person learns through the consequences of their behavior. The type of sales process you engage in will either induce prospects to engage with you, which is the desired behavior for you as the sales rep, or will cause them not to engage with you, which in your prospect's mind equals the removal of negative consequences.

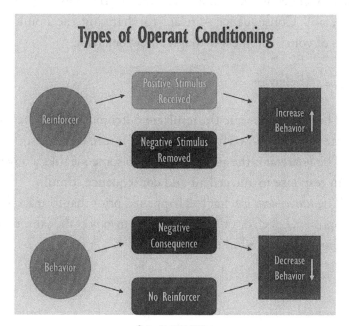

© Copyright 2017 Bill Hart

People behave based upon positive and negative reinforcements. They also perceive future situations based upon previous experiences. You engage in your sales calls in the same way. You engage based upon past experiences, unless something dramatic has caused you to change. People change behavior when reinforcement directs them toward that behavior. People avoid behavior when punishment is the result.

The key thing to note here is that with no feedback, positive or negative, the behavior declines. So, if you make a sales call and don't reinforce that call with a positive experience for the prospect, the positive reference or positive mindset toward you will fade away.

Good experiences need to be reinforced. In terms of sales, you need to reinforce, in the buyer's mind, that you deliver value. You need to do that a lot. Even after the sale, this point is important, for if an account is not properly nurtured, the favorable view of you will fade away.

The model below shows how the ABCs of Behavior – Antecedent, Behavior, and Consequence – relate to changing the opinions and behaviors of your customers through a new behavior.

The ABCs of Behavior[8]

- The *consequences* are the results or outcomes of the behavior and are the most powerful influence on future behaviors.
- The *behavior* is the action or reaction someone (like a buyer) has in response to antecedent and consequence stimuli.
- The *antecedent* is what has happened prior that forms a person's opinion, belief, or value. It makes them expect the same outcome they experienced in the past.

---

[8] Concepts and excerpts from the sales course *Grow Big: The Art of Non-Selling* by Bunnell Idea Group www.bunnellideagroup.com

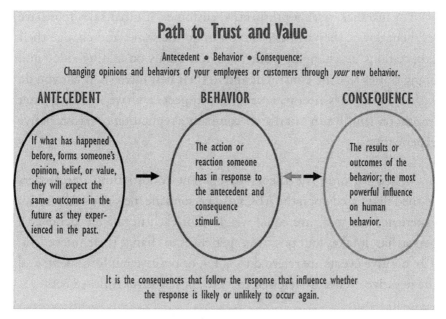

It is the consequences that follow the response that influence whether the response is likely or unlikely to occur again.

© Copyright 2017 Bill Hart

To change the consequences in your favor, you must understand the role the antecedent plays in your buyer's behavior. People's past experiences cause them to view an interaction with you in a certain light, with either positive, neutral, or negative expectations. It is their conditioning.

What happens in one situation conditions a person to expect the same outcome in future situations. Their experience conditions them to expect similar results in the future, and thus predetermines their reaction or behavior. Antecedents may even cause a person to misinterpret data and miss seeing reality. An antecedent is the lens through which a person might view a particular situation. Past failures will cause a person to avoid risk. Past successes will cause a person to be more of a risk taker.

Things you do can cause someone to respond favorably or unfavorably. The problem is that one good experience does not negate one negative experience. According to Skinner's research, it takes four positive experiences to negate one negative one!

For instance, with a prospective customer, if other sales reps have let them down, they will expect you to do the same. You change their expectations by changing your behavior. Focus on adding value and doing things that are consistent and in their best interest. What you do within 30-60 days after you meet the prospect can have a much greater impact on your future than your company's reputation or past negative experiences.

When forming the theory of operant conditioning, researchers learned that based upon the ABCs of a person's life, negative and positive experiences do not have equal weight. For each negative experience a person has, it takes four positive experiences to change their antecedent. The positive events are referred to as R+, or positive reinforcement; and the negative events are referred to as R-, or negative reinforcement.

Applying this 4:1 concept to sales, for every unpleasant experience your customer has, you must create four positive experiences to overcome it. If you are just meeting the customer's need with your product and service and are not focused on adding continual value, your revenue stream is at risk!

## No R+ puts your revenue stream at risk.

With every customer relationship, there will be challenges; it is just a part of doing business. If your problem-solving practices are reactive versus proactive, you are most likely creating more R- experiences rather than R+ experiences. A proactive and well thought-out problem-solving process can create an R+ for the customer.

# Operant Conditioning 4:1

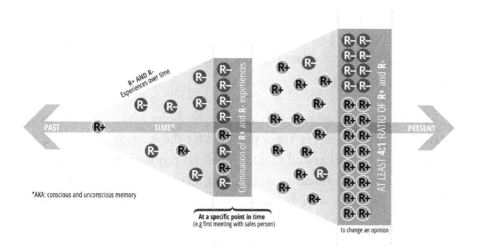

Let's apply the R+, R- concept to a sales call. Jane is a sales rep selling an expense tracking software system that centralizes expenses from branch offices into one central office, allowing better control over expenses and reduction of paperwork. Her company's software also allows the sales reps to be reimbursed in more quickly. Jane has been trying to get an appointment with Dave, the controller of a mid-sized IT services company that has several branches. Dave is hard to reach and never returns e-mails or phone calls. Jane works diligently to find a connection so she can get a referral to Dave. She eventually finds a mutual connection on LinkedIn and gets an introduction.

By referring Jane, this mutual friend is implying that Jane has something of value to offer, so Dave agrees to meet with her. Jane does not know that Dave has a history of unfavorable experiences with sales people. His first real experience in buying a big-ticket item was a car. The sales rep was pushy and talked too much. Dave's next experience was buying a home where the realtor did nothing but "show" the house. Dave had to do all the leg work and pushed the negotiations to close the deal. In his current position, most sales reps waste his time by going into a product presentation before his goals, needs, or a problem have been identified, and before they have demonstrated substantiated value. They also assume they already know his needs and his desired outcomes. From his experience, sales reps do not add value or offer anything different than what he can find by searching the Internet for new solutions or up-to-date pricing. Based upon the referral, Dave is hoping Jane is different.

In preparing for the meeting, Jane does her homework and researches Dave and his company, so she is prepared for the meeting. She engages Dave in a conversation and identifies several problems Dave has with his current expense tracking system and identifies what he wants for the future. She sees ways her software could increase efficiencies and solve a nagging problem with the current system. Jane does not try to sell anything to Dave. Dave has a few questions about the configuration and interoperability with his core accounting system. Jane says she will get back to him with the answers (but does not give a time frame). The meeting ends and Jane feels that she has a hot prospect.

Right after Jane leaves the meeting, she gets two calls from a customer who has some major problems. She spends two hours tracking down the solution. Now the day is over. She gets home and must solve two family issues while also having to plan her next day. Jane's next few days are full of problem-solving and working on a proposal she is late getting to a prospect. The next week Jane goes on vacation for a week.

Jane comes back from vacation and calls Dave to follow up. Dave does not return her phone calls. Jane sends an email with his questions answered, but Dave does not respond. Jane is perplexed about why Dave is no longer responsive after such a good meeting. Jane attempts several more times over the next month to "check in" to gage his interest. She finally reaches Dave on the phone, and he tells her that he decided not to pursue her solution and that she has no reason to call on him again.

What happened to Jane? Why did Dave seem so favorable in the beginning, then became so opposed? Dave's antecedent of R-s in dealing with sales reps was forming his opinion of Jane. Although she was prepared and the meeting went well, creating two R+, Jane did nothing to quickly add more R+ to differentiate herself from other sales reps. She did not follow up with value quickly. She got sidetracked into working on other things, thus proving to Dave that sales reps waste time and don't add value. Also, the more time passes before another positive event, R+, the less impact that event has in swaying a behavior. Jane let too much time lapse and lost the effect of her R+s on Dave.

## Plan your R+ Steps to building Trust.

There are several ways Jane could have added R+ after the sales call to build trust and altar Dave's perception. She could have:

1) Followed up immediately with a meeting summary email stating Dave's current business issues, problems, the proposed solutions, and the potential next steps. This would have communicated that Jane listened well; good listening skills add value and show the buyer that you care about them.

2) Sent a hand-written thank you card showing appreciation for his time. This would have showed that Jane knows Dave's time was valuable, and that she was making an extra effort to be different.

3) Connected Dave with someone who he would value meeting, thus creating value and trust.

4) Sent Dave an article on how others have addressed some of the challenges he faces. This would have shown that Jane had industry knowledge and was focused on solving Dave's problem.

5) Connected with Dave on LinkedIn, creating relationship network value.

6) Responded to Dave's questions within a week or established a timeframe that Dave agreed to and followed through. This would have demonstrated that Dave is important and that Jane can quickly follow through, thus giving Dave the expectation that she will respond promptly to his issues.

Jane's behavior following the meeting really could have solidified that she offers value and is really working to solve Dave's problems. She would have appeared to be doing more than just trying to sell him a product. An R+ experience after the meeting would have had a greater impact on Dave's perception of Jane than the initial meeting itself.

If you are a sales leader, teach your sales steps to create R+ experiences. If a rep cannot consistently add value, then it would be better for him to never call on the prospective customer rather than reinforce negative views and creating a negative opinion of your company.

Customers buy from vendors who create R+ experiences; they trust them. And providing cumulative R+ experiences with your customer encourages them to be more tolerant of an R- every now and then.

*"Being trusted is the single most urgent way to build a business."*
*-Seth Godin*

Here are two comments from a LinkedIn discussion group on sales and the value of building trust through R+ actions:

> "Even if you are totally truthful, guileless, and non-manipulative, as well as generous and benevolent, you WON'T get the fast trust you deserve. Another one of Seth's concepts applied to trust 'having your trust be REMARKABLE.' Otherwise your prospect doesn't KNOW you are those things – and it will tragically take you months of reference checks, little orders to test you, and other delays - because the prospect applies the stereotype to you, and assumes your truth telling is hype, 'just like other sellers.' I call the solution Radical Truth Marketing."

> -Ron Richards, Radical Truth Marketing.

Establishing trust and rapport is an obvious element of success (mandatory). I believe that this is established by consistent execution. How many people do you know that have good ideas... they are nothing unless you execute!"

-Scott Schaul, SVP of Savi Technology

I used this process of delivering R+ experiences to win one of my largest clients. This prospect had a physical therapy company and sold physical therapy software to other clinics around the world. To get an appointment with the CEO, I got a referral from a very respected influencer. I did my homework researching her company, her competition, and her bio on LinkedIn. I came to the appointment with an agenda, but the first thing I asked was, "Deborah, what do you want to accomplish during this meeting? How will you define this meeting as being successful?"

That question immediately showed that I was focused on her objectives and criteria. During the meeting, I took extensive notes and asked a lot of questions. She did most of the talking. A few stories were told, but I presented nothing. At the meeting's end, I summarized our conversation and asked if I missed anything. I told her that I would send a meeting summary to confirm what we covered. The purpose of this was to demonstrate that I was fully engaged in listening and that I truly understood her situation. This follows the axiom that people want to be heard and understood before they can hear and understand you.

I sent the meeting summary within 24 hours, and she received a hand-written card within 3 days. I followed up by sending her an article on Whole Brain˚ Thinking, in which she had expressed an interest.

In two weeks, we had a follow up meeting with 2 other employees evaluating me, for I had yet to officially present anything. I focused on listening to their needs and asked a lot of questions about their concerns related to sales questions. I summarized the meeting and sent a meeting summary plus a hand-written card to the two other employees.

When I finally made the proposal to Deborah, she informed me that the other companies she was considering were no longer in the running. I had eliminated the competition before I even got to the proposal. She implemented Customer Aligned Selling with her team. Within six months, referrals were up 150% and net profits were up 8%. Software sales rose 35% within 18 months.

# Chapter 7

## Four Components of the Buying Decision

In Chapter One, I mentioned the four components of the decision-making process. Now I want to go into these in more detail. The statistical data found in the process is important, as to where the emphasis of sales strategy and sales training is placed.

In his book, *Achieve Sales Excellence,* Howard Stevens explains the four components of the customer's decision-making process when selecting a vendor. The results of his research are determined from 80,000 customer interviews and 210,000 interviews with sales reps from 7,500 organizations over 14 years! Howard Stevens is CEO of Chally Assessments, an organization that approaches sales from a scientific standpoint (www.chally.com).

The four components of a buyer's decision and how important they are:

- Sales rep's competence    39%
- Total solution    22%
- Quality    21%
- Price    18%

Without a qualified and competent sales rep, the buyer never gets to the solution, quality, or price. And interestingly, price is the last thing negotiated. Too many sales leaders think price is paramount to the buyer because they are told by their sales reps that deals were lost because the price was too high. For the buyer, using price as the disqualifier is the easiest thing to say, and it may not necessarily be the true deciding factor. What the buyer may have been thinking was, "As a sales rep, you stink! You don't have a clue about my business or my needs. You are not adding value. All you do is talk and try to manipulate me with a lower price. I will string you along because I need three quotes, but you don't stand a chance at getting my business."

The rep says, "Boss, we lost the business because our price was too high." Did the rep really see the competitor's proposal? Not likely. In all probability, the competitor was higher. Companies that sell strictly on price generally lose to the company who focuses on sales rep competence, which not only trumps price, but also delivers higher margins, long-lasting business, and pleasant customers. If your sales strategy is to sell on price, I bet you have customers who don't value the other services you have to offer. Do you know the reason why these customers do not value what you have to offer? Go ask them. Most likely, by selling on price, you have told them that all the other benefits are not important, or are no different than the competition. By selling on price, your sales reps prove that there is no differentiation.

An easy example is automobile sales. Except for Cadillac, Lexus, Infinity and a few other high-end cars, almost all car dealers sell on price. They all claim differentiating features, but at the end of the commercial, they promote the lowest price. What was the last thing left in the car buyer's mind? Price, of course. When you go to a dealership to look at a car, you most likely have done your homework regarding features, pricing, and other data. In my personal experience purchasing nine cars, I have never had a sales rep engage me in a value-based discussion. Most of the time, all the sales rep does is show me a car, quote a price, and then hand me a business card and say, "Call me if you are interested." I bet I could get 10,000 of the same stories within a month if I requested car buying experiences on Facebook. For the auto industry, the Internet, which adds value, has replaced the role of the sales rep.

Another example is when the seller tries to win a deal by lowering their price. They use the lower price as a compelling (i.e. manipulative) reason to buy. The seller is dumbfounded when the buyer does not buy and goes with the more expensive option, or chooses to do nothing at all. Many times, the buyer claims the price was too high, but does not go with any solution offered, thus demonstrating that value was not established by any vendor.

<u>Why Sellers Sell on Price</u>

Sales reps sell on price for a few reasons, but one of the main justifications is fear: "What if I lose the sale?" Fear drives a sales rep to think illogically. Fear is increased when the prospect tells him or her that price is the only thing that will win the deal.

What drives the customer to focus on price? Typically, there are four scenarios:

- The vendor's management is focused on price, believing it is the main driver for a buying decision.
- The sales rep is not adding enough value in the relationship, or being a differentiator. There is no perceived added value in the buyer's mind. The sales rep has not understood the buyer's criteria in terms of tying the solution to the business impacts, increasing/protecting revenue, reducing/controlling expenses, or reducing/controlling risk. *The sales rep has not identified what or how the customer will determine the best solution, and therefore cannot present the customer with that offer.*
- The criteria of a competent sales rep, a specific solution, and the level of quality offered have no value to the customer. The added value does not fit within the customer's business objectives. For instance, your company's solution might be outside their budget

range (Chevy budget when looking at a Cadillac or BMW). The extra features do not add value in terms of impacting revenue, reducing/controlling expenses, or reducing risk.

- The risk of going with your company's solution is too great. The customer has to change from their current vendor to your company, where the implication of negative impact related to service, parts, people, and processes is huge.

## Focus on Price = No Difference

Most sales strategies and sales reps are still conditioning or "training" their own customers to buy on price. The sales rep brings up price in the discussion, and in so doing, makes the price the most important issue. **Price is where a customer goes when they cannot find any value**. The auto industry is a perfect example of this truth. If the rep understands this fact and does not lead with price, then the next sales effort is the "spray and pray" tactic, hoping that with all the features and benefits given, the buyer will figure out what fits. Unfortunately, hope is not a valid sales strategy. Few reps are trained to have a discussion around solutions: satisfying a need, solving a problem, or achieving a goal while tying it to revenue, expenses, or risk. World-class sales organizations develop their strategy and train their reps to understand how the customer wants to buy.

For consumer sales, revenue may not be the driver. Find that other reason: quality of life, growth of assets, enjoyment, image, better service, greater efficiency, and better health, for instance.

Is your organization struggling with sales? Are your reps taking 20 to 40% longer to close than they should? Have you cut costs to the bone, and now you need to increase sales, but more effort does not seem to work? Are you still selling on price when it is only 18% of the decision?

Many CEOs did not come from a sales background and therefore are not trained in these issues. Many Vice Presidents of Sales are above the age of 50. They remember how they were successful and try to replicate what they did, but their old sales strategy no longer works. Working longer hours or firing your sales reps is not an effective strategy - just ask the pharmaceutical industry!

World-class organizations understand what their customers want. They develop their reps to have the competence to help organizations improve effectiveness, save time, or reduce expenses and risk. Effective sales reps focus on helping their customer achieve effective outcomes. These organizations know that the sales rep's competence is 39% percent of the customer's decision in the buying process. Companies that are stuck in the 20th century sales model are still spending their marketing and sales dollars emphasizing a lower price, while trying to provide a better solution and the best quality. Little effort and money is spent on helping their sales reps become value providers to their customers. Many CEOs and VP of Sales do not believe they can truly change the sales process, since they see selling as an art that cannot be scientifically replicated. Thus, training resources are not effectively spent on making reps more effective, nor are the senior executives engaged in the training process. Instead, resources are spent on more product training, which by itself does not increase effectiveness.

Changes in Business Strategy

In the past thirty years, there have been different strategies that gave vendors or suppliers a competitive advantage. Let's continue to look at the automobile industry and how strategies and competitive differences have changed.

Price gave the Japanese car industry an advantage in the 1970s and 1980s, but you will not find a Japanese car less expensive than an American car today. Japanese quality was poor at first, but in the last 10 - 15 years, that quality has surpassed American and European cars. As the competition achieved price parity and worked to achieve quality parity, the auto manufacturers offered new features and solutions to their cars. American auto companies offered new ways to finance and new owner programs. To stay competitive, all the other car manufacturers had to eventually offer similar features, service, and/or financing.

For any auto manufacturer to even stay in the game in today's market, let alone make a profit, they must offer a competitive price, a quality product/service, and a total solution. What is left to differentiate any company from all the others? The sales rep's competence or price. Because car dealers have done such a poor job of meeting customer's needs i.e., the sales rep's competence, the Internet and financing are the two main value-adds for car dealers. Thus, the margins that car dealers previously enjoyed on new cars have dropped significantly. The auto dealers make those margins up in creative and high interest financing schemes, or in service/repair work.

## Management's Role and Control

There is another reason management focuses on quality, total solution, and price: they can control those components from their headquarters. Management can set or lower the price. They can implement ISO 9000 programs for quality and create total solutions by partnering with other companies, through buying another company, research and development, and/or adding to the product line. Management can create new offerings based upon customer needs. The majority of management's perspective is analytical, left-brain thinking.

From the typical manager's perspective, the sales function is viewed as an art or a skill, and not a science or a directly controllable process like manufacturing. In many cases, management sees salespeople as born with the gift of sales or persuasion: they either have the gift or they don't. Management can control what happens on the plant floor, but they can't control what happens on the sales floor - or so they think. So, management focuses on the factors they can control and understand, like operations, production, finance, and human resources. Many CEOs over the age of 50 climbed the company ranks through operations and finance, and do not truly understand sales, especially selling in the 21st century. If they do have a sales background, the world of sales has changed so much, it is typically not what they dealt with in their sales tenure.

Research on executives conducted by organizations such as Hogan Assessments, Brinkman, and Herrmann International reveal CEO personality and how they think. The typical CEO is strong in vision, analytics, and processes (cerebral and left-brain thinking), and is less interested in relationships, intuition and human interaction (right-brain thinking). According to Daniel Pink in *A Whole New Mind -Why Right Brainers Will Rule the Future*, successful organizations will need more right brain thinking. Sales involves a majority of right brain thinking.

## Right brain thinking is needed to be successful in selling.

Many executives try to win new business by focusing on improving the product or service they offer instead of focusing on the greatest asset the company has: its sales process. The process of getting the offering into the customer's hands or the customer's outcomes using the product or service is completely neglected! What little sales training is given to sales reps typically focuses on product features and benefits, or skills such as prospecting, presenting, negotiating, and closing. Zig Ziglar's *The Secret of Closing the Sale,* and *How to Master the Art of Selling* by Tom Hopkins are classic examples of such training.

Other types of training may be motivational in nature, such as developing a winning attitude and goal setting, which are done from the seller's perspective, and not from the buyer's. CEOs who did not come up through sales ranks do not readily see this as a problem; however, times have dramatically changed even for CEOs did. Unless they are currently making sales calls or are up to speed in engaging their customers, they are probably not fully aware or educated on how and why the customer's buying process has been transformed.

What worked for them no longer works today! Even the best-selling book on solution selling, *SPIN Selling* by Neil Rackham, Ph.D. psychologist (copyright 1988), is out of date. Rackham confirms that fact in *Selling Power* Magazine interviews and in live sessions. On his website, www. NeilRackham.com, he says that sales people must become *value creators.* In a session at a Sales Management Association conference in Atlanta in 2013, Rackham emphasized that creating value can be educating the customer on better ways or different ways of solving problems or achieving goals. The seller brings innovation from his experiences with other clients.

## Management's Role in Training

Senior management must understand what is important to the customer, as well as to the sales people. When I conduct sales training with organizations, I emphasize the importance of involving top management in the sales training. I readily get buy-in from the senior vice president or sales director that they will participate, but what happens in reality is different.

At the point in training where we cover human buyer behavior, we get to a critical point that cries for a change in the current sales process. The sales reps will look around and ask, "Where is John (i.e. the senior sales executive)? He needs to hear this. He is always telling us to do it the old way!" Unfortunately, the senior sales executive has left the room to solve a crisis or to pursue what he or she deems "more important." The sales reps feel that senior leadership is giving lip service to Customer Aligned Selling. When sales goals or quotas are not achieved, or problems with the sales process or delivering solutions arise, management may accuse the sales reps. "You guys aren't performing, and we paid for all that sales training." Many times, the trainer or the sales reps get blamed for poor or outdated sales methodologies. Real and lasting change must come from the top down. It cannot be mandated; it must be modeled!

I don't blame management for not attending the old style of sales training. There were a lot of legitimate reasons management did not attend such training, which focused on prospecting, presenting, and closing, and/or on product knowledge. That training offered them little value. They knew their products and were not in front of customers trying to close. These senior leaders viewed the old sales training merely as a technical skill they already knew. Participating in training was not time well spent. But times have changed and so have customers. Today, customers require senior leaders to be actively involved in larger deals, so they need to have the same skills as their sales reps.

I believe many senior managers do not give Customer Aligned Selling top priority because subconsciously, they think selling is a skill that applies to prospecting and closing the deal. Many senior leaders do not understand what the customer expects from their supplier, and, in some cases, does not believe there is anything new to learn. If senior management really wanted to know what the customer expects, they would be in the field with the sales reps meeting customers. Kudos to you senior leaders who do make sales calls and regularly talk with your customers!! You know that your activities pay huge dividends.

Successful sales organizations have leaders who are engaged and are making sales calls. There is a huge emphasis within world class sales organizations to make sales a cross-functional tactic, getting everyone who interfaces with the customer involved in the sales process.

Questions

- Is delivering value a regular topic of management meetings?
- Is the majority of the sales training product-related?
- Do the senior level executives actively participate in training?
- Does management see the sales function as a means to manipulate revenue?
- When was the last time your CEO went on a normal sales call (i.e. not a super high profile, "make it or break it," prospect)?

- If you are a senior sales leader, when was the last time you asked your customers why they bought from you?
- If you are a senior leader/business owner who goes on calls, asks a lot of questions, and listens to your customer, well done! You are a great role model for your team.

# Chapter 8

# The Sales Rep's Competence

For most organizations, transitioning to a Customer Aligned Selling model is not easy. They have been doing business a certain way for a long time. It is hard to swallow that what you learned and what has made you successful for the past five, 10, or 20 years, may no longer work. Your people might think, "Information technology, the Internet, social media, and social change are great… as long as it does not require me to change my business model."

Our past and the way we think can be the greatest limitations we face in achieving change and aligning our organizations with the way customer's buy. The exercise below demonstrates that those greatest limitations can be self-imposed from the way we were taught and from our experiences in life.

Connect the stars using 4 straight lines **without** lifting your pen from the page. The key is you cannot lift your pen once you begin drawing the lines. Note that a line is straight, not curved as some have tried to change the rules.

```
    *           *           *


    *           *           *


    *           *           *
```

I almost always know what the first response is. This exercise plays to the way we were taught from a very early age when learning to draw or write, i.e. connect the dots to form the picture or letter. You were ingrained from age three to connect the dots in a normal, structured, or inside the box method. Psychologists tell us that our minds group things and put parameters around items to create organization and structure, so I was using your conditioned mind against you.

When you began to do this exercise, your brain had you immediately connecting the dots in a row and together within a box. I bet you tried multiple times to connect the dots and even lifted your pen. Many people even draw a curved line to connect them. Every time I give this exercise, only one or two people out of a group of 20 will try to connect the dots outside of the "box" the dots form. The rest are stuck in their "box" of dots. The whole page is open to them, but due to the way we have learned, they do not try a new approach. Many give up. I have had multiple people tell me it is impossible.

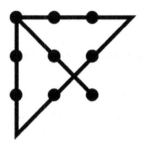

Now, connect the dots with two lines not lifting your pen.

*

                              *

                              *

*

It is easy once you go beyond your self-imposed limitations.

At the beginning of this chapter you read that the greatest limitations can be self-imposed or are related to our past. Does that statement trigger or evoke a logical or emotional response? Typically not. If people have experienced this before, they will agree, but most people just stare blankly or nod their heads. Regarding connecting the dots, I find it funny that people will tell me that's cheating or that I did not explain it that way, for it is their minds that are limiting them, not me. Their minds are boxing them in instead of looking for new answers. A few times, I will have someone ask me, "Can I look on someone else's paper?" or "I have the answer; can I help others?" My answer is always, "Yes." I never said the group could not work on the problem as a whole, or that people could not help each other.

Many times, when one person wants help, another participant

will protest: "That's cheating," or "That's not fair." People make a simple learning exercise, business project, or even serving the customer a competition within their own organization.

So, what does this exercise have to do with the sales rep's competence? Everything! The sales rep must be retrained to focus on adding value at every step of the sales process. Remember, a good sales process *is* the sale! The company, from senior leadership, operations, and sales, to customer service; all must understand what the customer needs and demands. For many, this means learning to connect the dots in a whole new way, entering new space and approaching sales from a different perspective: *the customer's perspective.*

## The Seven Rules of the Customer

In the book *Achieve Sales Excellence,* Howard Stevens set forth the seven rules of the customer from conducting 80,000 customer interviews. Neil Rackham's research with Xerox, IBM, and other companies with over 1500 sales transactions, agrees with Steven's research. From my own anecdotal experience, they are right on the money. And, if you learn and apply these seven rules in your sales processes, you will succeed.

To truly understand and apply the full meaning and impact of these rules, I highly recommend studying *Achieve Sales Excellence,* not just reading it. If you are a senior leader, the last section of Steven's book asks eight questions for identifying world class sales organizations. These are some direct and tough questions, but ones that should be addressed. Your analysis will help you assess whether you are in the 20$^{th}$ or 21$^{st}$ century; in terms of your sales strategy and processes.

To truly understand why these 7 rules are so important, in the research customers reported that there are 4 main criteria used when selecting a vendor and the percentage weight in making a buying decision.

- Sales Rep's competence    39%
- Total Solution    22%
- Quality    21%
- Price    18%

Seeing that the sales rep's competence surpasses all other criteria for the customer in making a buying decision, it is imperative that a sales rep and sales leaders understand the seven rules that the customer expects a sales rep to know and apply.

As a refresher, the seven rules of the customer are:

- You must be personally accountable for our results.
- You must understand our business.
- You must be on our side.
- You must bring us applications – not just products.
- You must be easily accessible.
- You must solve our problems.
- You must be innovative in responding to our needs.

Rule #1: "You must be personally accountable for our results."

Sales people who understand Customer Aligned Selling take personal responsibility for the customer's results. These reps' foremost concern is that the customer achieves the best solutions; the results that they expected and paid for. These reps act as business agents, or as outsourced managers who are responsible for all aspects of the relationship with the buyer. They act as the single point of contact within their organization to ensure the buyer receives the right resources and communication. They may delegate some activities, but not responsibility. They are responsible for the client's outcome, and the client knows it. This is known as outcome ownership, and it is the path to making your customers raving fans.

Rule #2: "You must understand our business."

To personally manage the relationship, a sales rep must truly understand the customer's business. This involves not only understanding the customer, their organization, culture, competencies, and business strategy, but also their industry, current trends, financial and economic pressures, and even competition. It means seeing the customer's business as their CEO sees the business.

Rule # 3: "You must be on our side."

To truly serve your customer, you must see things from their perspective, and then represent your customer's point of view back to your company. Your job is to make sure that in your company's quest for profit and efficiency, your customer's perspective is not forgotten. You keep your company from alienating your customer. In understanding your customer's perspective, you must be aware that their perspective is the only one that matters to them. You must also be aware of vested interests in your company that do not benefit the customer, and work around them. Lastly, your advocacy for your customer is most valid when your customer is not present. You must represent them at all times.

Rule #4: "You must bring us applications."

Customers want substantiated value at every step of the sales process. Substantiated value does not mean presenting features and benefits and hoping the buyer understands how they will help them. Bringing applications means the sales rep can discuss the product's usage, outcomes, or results of using that product. Your customer wants to know how your offering applies to their particular need and how it can be implemented to produce the desired results. The sales rep's skill must be in creating a match between the seller's offerings and the buyer's situation, thus bringing them applications.

Rule #5: "You must be easily accessible."

The average sales person spends a small amount of time in actual contact with customers. In several studies, actual direct time with customers was less than 25%, and that included problem-solving. In today's world, every company should have a defined process for keeping in touch with the customer, from automated email responses and 24-hour call back rule, to problem escalation and communication rules, even texting. The key for the customer is the level and quality of response. Good communication is key. What causes stress for a customer is a sense of being out of control and not having the right information to regain control.

Rule #6: "You must solve our problems."

What makes great sales people is their anticipation of problems and their solutions. These problems can be caused by their company, by the customer, or by some other factor. Great sales reps have the mindset of a troubleshooter. They equip themselves to deal with problems in advance. They see problem solving as a positive challenge and a valuable opportunity: R+ opportunities. The sales person remains personally responsible for the resolution; they do not delegate the final responsibility to someone else.

Rule #7: "You must be innovative to responding to our needs."

Customers want their supplier or service provider to be continuously improving the offering throughout the relationship. Executives want salespeople who can keep them up to date on innovative new solutions that addresses strategic challenges and provide new opportunities for improving their company's sales, reducing costs, or growing profits. Executives want salespeople to be up-to-date and ongoing learners. They want to ensure there is added value in a relationship, and not just what the sales rep's company offers at that moment. This requires sales reps to understand the industry, to be subject matter experts, to understand the customer's competition, and to search for innovative ideas in other industries. Innovation comes from extensive reading and from having a broad network of contacts in different industries.

# Chapter 9

## Different Perspectives

How many squares do you see?

Below is a block of squares. Write at the bottom of the page how many squares you see. You will find the answer given on the following page. Do the exercise and then read the chapter. Do not just speed read through to find the answer, or skip doing this exercise. See if you can really find the correct number. Too many times people want the answer without going through the process. Going through the process and struggling to see a new perspective – in this case, to see new squares - is how you learn. By just finding the answer, you short-cut yourself and do not experience new perspectives. Not understanding a new perspective is where many sales organizations are stuck, and the customers are paying for it, or in reality, not paying.

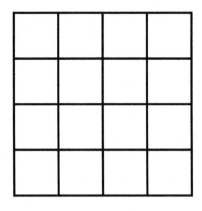

The rules have changed in the sales/marketing process. Selling has changed dramatically over the last few decades, primarily because customers have changed:

- Most customers are far more knowledgeable about products and services available today than ever before.
- According to many sources from IDC and Gartner Group, 50% or more of the decision to buy a product or service is made before the prospect ever contacts the seller.
- Competition is far stronger and more determined than it has ever been.
- There are more products and services available to satisfy the customer's needs than ever before.
- Customers are more sophisticated and demanding than they have ever been, even regarding the smallest products.
- Customers depend upon factors other than product understanding to make a buying decision.

Most of old style selling was the climax of the close. All the selling skills were focused on identifying a need or creating a desire, then bringing the customer to a decision to buy. The focus was on the transaction. This was the focus of solution selling – identify the need or pain, match your solution to the need, and close.

Today's focus must be on bringing value to the relationship - using systems and processes that best serve the customers. From the customer's perspective, nothing happens until after the close. The customer is buying an outcome. The sales transaction is just a step in the process of fulfilling a need, achieving a goal, or finding a solution to a problem. The customer goes through the transaction to get to a solution. *Every **person** in the seller's company should understand this fundamental principal.* From the customer's perspective, the whole sales process, from beginning to solution delivery, is the cumulative reason to buy.

## The customer is buying an outcome. That is the focus of the sales process.

The squares exercise is used to demonstrate that helping your customer may require seeing the situation from their perspective or using the sales process to empower them to see a new perspective. Not only are sellers stuck in the way they do business, but many customers/buyers are also stuck (seeing only 24 or 26 squares). One of the skills in Customer Aligned Selling is helping that buyer see a new perspective – i.e. seeing new squares they had not seen before. This requires executives and sales reps to be open to new ideas, and to be constantly sharing what they learned in a meaningful way that brings value to their client. This is the Challenger Sales concept.

There are 30 squares – single squares, double, and triple sets.

Vendor Perspective

From the vendor or supplier's perspective, the 16-21 squares you easily see is how business is approached on a day-in and day-out basis. Vendors rank accounts from tertiary to strategic depending on the size and volume of business. The more strategic the account, the more the vendor attempts to align their business processes with them. The focus is typically on technical and strategic aspects related to inventory or financing. In most cases, there is little attention given to how the customer wants to buy (squares 24-27) or what new solutions the customer might need (squares 28-30).

Most vendors or suppliers are organized from a hierarchical perspective of sales, operations, and customer service. They are managed from a vertical perspective that does not focus on what the customer wants or needs. Quotas and forecasts drive sales efforts (quarterly, semi-annual, or annual), with the focus on increasing stock value or making the senior executives high salaries. For public companies, Wall Street drives the quarterly forecast, and not the buying customer. This shareholder-driven process stifles the progress from customer service to the company's bottom line. Sales organizations that base their forecasts and quotas upon Wall Street may give up a lot of margin, work harder for less profit, and have more stress! Their customers understand this fact, and they use this high stress to their advantage by negotiating a lower price during the last week of each quarter. The customer has been trained by the seller to hold out to the end of the quarter, or end of the year, to get a lower price.

## Are you training your customers to hold out to a lower price based upon your quotas?

In my years selling IT software and services, I observed that Computer Associates in particular was notorious for dropping price to meet forecasts. Knowing that practice of dropping price, buyers would wait until the last month to negotiate a deal. From a consumer standpoint, for you to get the best deal, go buy a car the last day of the month with cash and see how much they will cut price.

Customer's Perspective

With the help of IT, strategic sourcing, more competition, and leaner work forces, businesses have focused on reducing their internal operational costs. One of the significant ways of cutting costs is limiting the number of suppliers or vendors with which a company deals. With fewer suppliers, the company can utilize IT systems and the Internet to leverage the relationships for better volume-based pricing and preferential treatment. Suppliers are willing to do this to lock up the business. Much time is required to select a strategic vendor, and suppliers know this. So, once a supplier is "in," a lot of bad (R-) has to happen for them to be fired. But suppliers are regularly fired for not meeting the customer's needs, understanding their business, and providing solutions that are relevant.

Customers buy products and services to use them. Features and benefits mean nothing until the product or service is used. The sales transaction, and even selecting a strategic supplier, is about getting results. Too many sales reps (and executives) forget this fact. Many times, buyers view the buying process as a necessary evil and treat sales reps disrespectfully, especially employees from the purchasing department. It is difficult for a sales rep to deal with such a buyer, but at times, they must. When possible, the better reps circumvent the price-only buyer and find the highest-level user – the manager or executive who will benefit from using the product or service – and engage in conversations related to the usage and outcomes of their product or service. Find where the buck stops and then make a connection. But, be sure you are talking about how they will use your product or service and how it helps achieve their desired outcomes. Talking features and benefits versus usage and outcomes is a sure way to get sent back to the purchasing department.

## A discussion of how a product or service is used relates to outcome.

Usage and Outcomes

Michael Bosworth and John R. Holland write of this topic extensively in the book, *Customer Centric Selling.* Usage scenarios are simply hypothetical examples that are highly relevant to the buyer and which you can use to conduct intelligent conversations.

Here are the success steps that focus on engaging in a discussion around usage.

1. Drop *starting with a presentation.* Starting with a presentation leads to discussing price because there is no value established, nor does the buyer see how your solution will be used within their company. A sales rep must get to business need before he/she can present. Since they don't know how to use your product or offering within their company

yet, they try to find a connection through price. If they can envision usage and outcomes, price is a minor issue!

2.   Understand that the sales process doesn't begin until the prospect has shared a problem or a goal. You don't have a qualified prospect until this happens.

3.   Engage in a discussion with the buyer which corresponds to the buyer's level in the company; the higher up in the organization, the less technical the conversation. The discussion should focus on achieving goals, solving problems, satisfying needs, and impacting revenue, expenses, and risk.

> a.   Senior people will send you down the chain if you speak language they don't understand or speak the language of a subordinate.
> b.   Use how and what questions.
> c.   Know their business or industry via the Internet.

Ask about specific goals related to their position, for example:

- CEO – growth, return on equity, and return on assets.
- COO – growth, operations, customer retention, and no downtime.
- CFO – protection of assets, return on investment, and cash flow.
- General Manager – reduction of waste, less downtime, increased and productivity.
- VP of Sales – increased gross margin, reduced sales cycle, increased revenue.

Do not make a presentation until a goal, a problem, or a need has been shared and you know the business impact. A presentation should be in the form of a discussion.

Create a vision of using your product or service; use examples in their business and relate it to them.

4.   Go slow – you are familiar with your offerings, but the buyer is not. Spend extra time discussing their need and creating a vision. Don't tell the buyer that you have a solution, let him tell you that you have a solution. This point is critical. Telling the buyer that you have a solution is arrogant. You may relate what you did for other clients and discuss how that solution may relate to their business, and then ask if that solution would work for them. The key word is to ***discuss,*** not tell.

5.   Leading with features counts on the buyer knowing whether or not the feature is useful and therefore relevant.

6.   Target your discussions around what the customer can DO <u>with</u> the product, and not what the product can do for them. This is the idea of using the product or service to achieve a specific outcome. For instance, if you are selling soft-serve ice cream machines, discuss with the business owner about how many customers your product can serve per hour in a specific situation, such as Friday night during the summer. If you are selling a 2-sided grill to a hamburger restaurant, engage in a discussion about crowd volume and customer wait times on Friday night and how 2-sided cooking can enable him to serve more customers in the same amount of time which increase profitability per hour (less labor and more burgers served).

If selling Electronic Medical Records (EMR) software, discuss with the doctor about how he currently interacts with his current EMR software and the 5 steps it takes him to record a patient visit. Then ask him to imagine doing that in 3 steps with your EMR and ask him what impact that would have on his daily productivity.

7.   Describe your offerings using verbs, not nouns. Using verbs helps the prospect envision using the product which creates ownership versus being told how it will benefit them. If a buyer feels like he/she is

being "sold," they will defend their position with objections. You can prevent objections by engaging the buyer in how the usage will meet their needs, achieve goals, or solve a problem.

For instance, a usage discussion regarding new expense software would focus on addressing how it could be used to solve the problems or issues involved. "Mr. Buyer, you have multiple offices, and everyone submits expenses in a manual format. When everyone electronically submits their expenses and the totals are summarized, how would having that feature impact your department's productivity? Would using such a process allow you to shift staff to different functions? How would centralizing expense reporting help you control expenses at the branch level?"

If the buyer has not answered sufficiently, the sales rep should share a story instead of telling about the benefits. "Mr. Buyer, may I share how one of our clients used our software to consolidate their expense reporting and the results they received?" The rep would then share the story and ask, "Do you see yourself achieving similar results, and how?"

The key word to use is "share," not "tell." Ask permission before going into a story. Be polite; honor them in the process. Your goal is to get them envisioning how they will benefit so they will tell you that your solution would work.

The Science of the Brain

In the book, *Resolved: 13 Resolutions for Life*, author Orrin Woodward discusses how brain research shows that the brain engages about 2 million neurons when discussing something. But when a person uses their imagination, the brain engages 400 million neurons. When imagining, the brain sees what it imagines as reality, so when conversing with a buyer, do it in terms of what can be and use positive words that cause them to envision your product or service getting the desired results. That is what usage scenarios do.

## Get the prospect to envision using your product or service.

Below is a worksheet you can use to relate your features to how a customer will use your product or service and their desired outcomes, as well as their possible buying criteria.

Here is a chart that can be used to map your features and benefits to usage, decision criteria, and desired outcome.

| Feature | Benefit | Usage | Outcome | Criteria for decision | Evidence needed |
|---------|---------|-------|---------|----------------------|-----------------|
|         |         |       |         |                      |                 |
|         |         |       |         |                      |                 |
|         |         |       |         |                      |                 |
|         |         |       |         |                      |                 |

On the next page is an example one of my clients in the restaurant equipment business did. He created this worksheet for one of the new double-sided grills.

| Feature | Benefit | Usage | Outcome | Criteria for decision | Evidence needed |
|---|---|---|---|---|---|
| Touchscreen Controls | Ease of Use Comfort of employees using equipment properly | Employees are used to using touchscreen, ease of use for employees | Less mistakes, happy employees | Current Equipment with touchscreens? | Employees engaged cooking with the controls – ease of use |
| Programmable Controls | Reduces Human error. Serve the same product to everyone | Programs are set & employees just have to select item to be cooked and hit start | Consistent product, reduced waste, variety of items on menu | Do you currently have a consistent product? | Demonstrate several programs where multiple cooks create the same recipe |
| Automatic Calibration | Consistent Product Less Waste Consistent Cook times | No need to adjust programming, the machine does it itself | Consistent product every time | Are you having to calibrate equipment, or having trouble staying consistent? | Time 4 different cooking scenarios |
| Precise Automatic Gapping | " | Calibrated grill will automatically adjust to ensure gap is the same every time. | Peace knowing that a consistent product is going to be served. | Consistently-cooked burger | Cook 4 burgers |
| Cooking Zones | Cook multiple items at a time on the same cook top. | 3 cooking zones with etched zones for proper placement of items. | During rush periods, it is easy to keep up, and will not have to run whole grill during slow times. | What do you currently do to cook multiple items? | Demonstrate eggs, burgers and toasting bread |
| Fault Log | You will be able to track your down time. | Faults in the program are recorded to ensure technician can fix grill ASAP | Less down time. More product being served. $$$ | Do you have problems with service now? | Data reports from others showing logs and downtime |
| Multi-function Mode | Grill has no limits to what you can cook and serve your customers | Employee can be told to turn, sear, season or melt cheese through programming. | Consistent product that you will be proud to serve to your customers. | Are there items on your menu where you can see this being useful? | Demonstrate multi-functions |
| Standby Alert | Can reduce operating energy by up to 40% compared to full time operation | Machine alerts employee to put into standby mode after a set idle time. | In standby, during slower times, up to 40% savings on operating energy. | Expensive energy bills can be reduced without compromising your operation. | Compare energy bill from an existing customer |
| External USB Port | Easily upload new menu items or promotional items to all stores. | Menu's or promotional items can be uploaded by USB | Get promotional items on the menu quick. Update grill menu easily | Do you have any experience with this kind of technology? | Upload menus |

From the customer's perspective, the decision to buy is not an isolated one. It involves not only purchasing, but also every department to be affected. Purchasing decisions, once isolated, have evolved into integrated decision-making processes that can have a broad impact across departments. More decisions are now made by committee or are made higher up in an organization. There has been a huge movement up the ladder in decision making. Ten years ago, a general manager, division manager, or controller could make purchasing decisions. Now, those decisions must be approved by a vice president, COO, CFO, or CEO.

If a senior level executive is making the decision, do you think he or she is interested in features and benefits? The executive is interested in outcomes and how your product or service will help them achieve this specific outcome. Few executives are tolerant of reps spouting outcomes that other clients received without doing the due diligence to find out what the specific issues or goals are with their company. Executives do not want the opinion of a sales rep. They want to discuss how the product or service will be used, and then they will tell you the outcome. The executive is concerned with his or her opinion, not the sales rep's - unless the sales rep has reached the position of trusted advisor[9] and the executive is a raving fan.

In conclusion, the old way of selling – focus on the transaction and getting paid – is in direct conflict with the buyer's goal, which again is to use the product or service for a solution that will improve or protect revenue, reduce or control expenses, and reduce or control risk. The old way of selling is failing since the Internet has eliminated much of the need for product demonstration or technical brochures. The old way of selling was to prospect, present features and benefits, focus on the close, and handle objections. Use an old familiar technique and you will alienate the buyer.

---

[9] "Trusted advisor" and "raving fan" are terms from the book *Raving Fans* by Ken Blanchard.

The new sales process is a beauty contest. This process does the closing for you, and the close begins and ends with *value*. The customer wants to have a positive experience throughout the whole process, from first contact to the last implementation. In summary, the whole sales process, from beginning to end, is what closes the deal.

## The whole sales process of adding value is the new "closing" technique.

Assess your sales effectiveness with these questions:

- Have you ever had a discussion with your top customers on why they do business with you?
- Does your company have a quarterly forecast where the emphasis is on making the numbers to keep the stock price high?
- Does your sales training include how to read an annual report, problem solving skills, or how to listen? Or does the majority of your sales training revolve around product knowledge, features, and benefits?
- Do you expect your sales reps to do a lot of cold calling?
- Are you training your customers to wait for a price cut?
- Who in your organization needs to read this chapter?
- Did you do the 30 Squares exercise? If not, you may be just reading this book in a *transactional* mode, i.e. get through the book and attain knowledge. If you did the exercise, you are entering the *transformational* mode, where you are willing to learn new ideas, and challenge the old way of selling.

Times have changed. Have you or your organization made the change, or are you struggling?

# Chapter 10

# What Makes Sales Happen: Trust

Sales happen when the customer trusts you, your product or offering, and your company. They trust that the price they are paying will return the value they are seeking. Trust forms the foundation for everything you do in business and in your personal life. Trust is truth, sincerity, perceived value, history of success, and the other person's confidence in you.

> *People decide on you or your sales reps before*
> *they decide on your solution or your company!*

What are the qualities or characteristics of people you trust?

- _____
- _____
- _____
- _____
- _____

The challenge with selling in today's market is that buyers have become very skeptical because so many promises have been broken. There is little trust. Our society has a trust issue not only in business, but also in relationships. For too many, the ends justify the means, or the current situation justifies breaking a promise. Two good examples are the divorce rate and the political landscape. To really delve into this subject, I recommend reading Jeffery Gitomer's book, *The Little Teal Book of Trust* and *The Speed of Trust* by Steven M. R. Covey.

Here are some key points about trust:

- You must first trust yourself. "Self-trust is the first secret of success." -*Emerson.*
- To trust is to take a risk for a perceived value.
- Trust is earned, not automatic.
- Trust is built upon cumulative events.
- You must consistently do things to build trust.
- You must consistently add value, R+ experiences. Having a good meeting on a sales call is not enough; timely follow-through is required.
- Trust is easily lost, especially due to complacency or self-centeredness.

Below are characteristics of trustworthiness. This exercise comes from the *Little Teal Book of Trust* by Jeffery Gitomer. You and your sales team should rate yourselves on a scale of 1-5 for each statement.

1= never 2= rarely 3= sometimes 4= frequently 5= all the time

| | |
|---|---|
| People rely on me. | 1 2 3 4 5 |
| When someone gives me a job to do, it's always done on or ahead of time | 1 2 3 4 5 |
| When someone gives me a job to do, it's always done to the best of my ability. | 1 2 3 4 5 |
| I have a reputation for getting the job done no matter what. | 1 2 3 4 5 |
| I am always on time. | 1 2 3 4 5 |
| I am dependable. | 1 2 3 4 5 |
| I am honest. | 1 2 3 4 5 |

| | |
|---|---|
| I tell the truth always. | 1 2 3 4 5 |
| When people trust me with a secret, they know their secret is safe. | 1 2 3 4 5 |
| When people trust me with matters of money, they know their money is safe. | 1 2 3 4 5 |

This test is not specifically for scoring purposes. It is more for self-awareness. If your score is high, it's most likely you are trustworthy. If your score is made of 3s and 4s, you are on the edge. And if your score is a made of 2s and 3s, you are probably not very trustworthy.

Here are some steps to build trust during the sales meeting:

- Come prepared; have an agenda and a goal for the meeting.
- State the meeting purpose and get your customer's goal for the meeting.
- Engage your audience in discussion.
- Have a conversation, not a presentation.
- Follow the 80/20 rule – your customer speaks 80% of the time.
- Ask questions, be a good listener and remember that telling isn't selling, asking is.
- Practice your questions before the meeting.
- Think about how you will be actively listening. Are you planning to take notes?
- Have a follow-up plan and communicate it.

Here are some more steps that build trust:

- Blogging on your industry issues demonstrates competence and trust.
- Doing what you say immediately shows integrity.
- Being on time helps foster a relationship of integrity and trust.
- Giving a gift and sending hand-written thank you cards helps build a relationship of trust.

- Consistent follow-up with meeting summaries demonstrates integrity and competence.
- Connecting customers with another person of value show competence and builds trust.
- Sending articles that are of interest to your prospect shows competence and builds relationship and trust.
- Doing something for their children or family builds relationship trust.

## What's Important to the Customer

Until you become a trusted advisor, and until the customer becomes a raving fan, the buyer-seller relationship is very one-sided from each person's perspective. The seller wants to make a sale, and the buyer could care less about the seller's need to make the sale. The seller is thinking, "It's all about my sales goal." The buyer is thinking, "You better listen to me if you want my business." In most cases, the sales rep is not listening, but is using old sales techniques of promoting products, features and benefits, manipulating with closing techniques, or just using the concept of *hope* as a sales strategy. With this type of relationship, the seller is hoping to make a sale while the buyer is hoping there is a diamond in the rough in all the presentations and opinions (this is also called the "spray and pray" technique). Unfortunately, this is the situation in most sales scenarios, from buying a car or construction equipment, to a drug rep calling on a physician, to interviewing a lawyer to hire.

## Why Consultative or Solution Selling Falls Short

With the consultative sales process, the goal is still to get to the transaction. The methodology of how to get to the transaction has changed: consult rather than present. Find the buyer's pain points before giving a solution, but the end game is still the same: to make a sale. Consultative selling does not train the sales rep to understand the buyer from their perspective, which is fundamental. Consultative selling may work in the short run because it does identify the buyer's pain and then sells a solution. Consultative sales training possesses some of the hallmarks of Customer Aligned Selling, but it still needs to move from a transactional focus to an outcome-based and futuristic approach. It is about seeing the customer's pain from the customer's perspective and understanding the needed outcomes from the customer's perspective. Customer Aligned is adding value beyond just solving a problem or satisfying a need. Ultimately, if the customer achieves the desired outcome, then consultative selling is in alignment.

Customer Aligned Selling goes beyond just understanding the buyer's need or goals. The Customer Aligned sales rep is thinking innovation, bring something new and empowering to their customer. This rep may identify needs that were not spoken, or even re-define the need to address the core issue, and then connect the dots to solving multiple problems and helping them exceed their goals. This rep not only understands the product or service, but personally adds value through his/her business acumen. The rep is the value-add, not just the product or service offering.

A client of mine, Sherry, sells inbound marketing services using HubSpot. Her specialty is creating content and special media campaigns to bring leads to a client's website. I gave her a referral to one of my clients. She identified his need for a more effective website that attracts more warm leads. They also needed a process to track the leads. HubSpot does all that. As she talked with the business owner, she probed for information that went beyond his marketing needs learning about his annual sales goals and the specific goals for each product line. Once she uncovered the inbound marketing need, she did not go to presentation mode of what HubSpot offers. Instead she asked more questions related to their overall sales process and how the sales reps follow up on inbound leads. By being patient and having the business owner share his current situation versus going for the obvious need, she uncovered that he also needed a new CRM and training for his sales reps. She discovered that part of his decision criteria is a seamless integration of the inbound marketing platform to the CRM, which is a HubSpot strength. She also found that ease of use and sales rep acceptance of the CRM platform was key to him buying.

Her follow-up was on building trust and validating the value of the sales call. She sent a meeting summary covering all his issues and potential solutions. The meeting summary demonstrated that she listened well and that the business owner was heard. She sent a hand-written thank you note which demonstrated her belief that the relationship was important. She also sent articles on how using inbound marketing is more effective in creating qualified leads versus cold calling, addressing one of his challenges in getting new customers. Her goal was to educate the business owner in the process, helping him make better decisions. The evidence he needed was success stories from other clients. She offered several references for him to call. To gain the sales rep's acceptance, they downloaded the free version and had the reps use it for a month.

Sherry's focus was on bringing innovation and empowering the customer to achieve his goals, thus she slowed down in her sales process and asked a lot more questions. She worked on making the buying process a valuable experience for the business owner versus just focusing on closing the sale. By doing so, she uncovered multiple goals and the gaps in achieving those goals. Her sale ended up being larger than expected, and the business owner was happy that he only has to deal with one company for marketing and CRM; a win for both sides.

As mentioned in the last chapter, what is important to the customer is the whole buying process. **The value-added sales process is the sale!** A Customer Aligned sales process is designed to:

a) Understand the customer's needs.
b) Possibly redefine those needs to better align with their goals.
c) Focus on the specific situation.

d) Relate usage to their business requirements and uncover new possibilities.

e) Understand and present to their desired decision criteria.

f) Focus on the desired outcomes (how they can solve a problem or achieve a goal).

**Customer Aligned Selling Process**

© Copyright 2017 Bill Hart

If all of the above is implemented, then the seller is truly focusing on what's important to the customer. The customer wants the whole buying process to be informative, customized to their situation, focused on them and on their goals, and flexible to their situation. And at every step, the sales rep should strive to add value.

## Value vs. Relationship

Because a buyer wants/needs value at every step of the sales process, a sales rep should be thinking about how he or she can add value at every step of the process, even when solving problems. Sales executives should be asking, "Are my people truly adding value, or just making sales calls with features and benefits presentations?" The number one question every sales rep should ask is, "How can I add value to this person, to this company, and to every step of the buying process?"

## The focus of adding value trumps the focus of building relationship.

Unfortunately, most sales reps are thinking, "How can I build a better relationship with this prospect or client so they will like me and do business with me?" The emphasis of most sales people is to build relationships and to be likeable. The rep thinks that the more he or she gets to know the buyer, the more the buyer will like them. They will also know more about the buyer's needs and problems. The latter part is partially true, but what today's buyers want is value. As mentioned, value leads to trust. When a buyer trusts you, they will allow you to build relationship. Once they allow time for relationship, he or she will begin to develop a friendship. And yes, it is true - people do business with those they like. But, in today's market, to get "liked," you are required to be a value provider. A value provider develops relationships where he or she becomes a trusted advisor. Then the buyer becomes a raving fan, and a true friendship is solidified. Buyers today are too busy to allow sales reps time to build relationship first, and then hope there is value in what the rep has to offer.

How to Add Value

Remember that adding value leads to trust. For your sales rep to add value, they must be continual learners. For a company to add value, the leadership team must be continual learners. I have heard it said that you are no different tomorrow from today, except for the books you read and the people you meet. To add value, one must be reading a lot of material. I read books on sales, books on leadership, plus industry related articles. I set a goal to read 20 books a year, and I have achieved that goal for the past seven years. Being well-read allows me to offer new perspectives to my clients (the emphasis of the Challenger sales model). My reading sharpens my mind to look for new opportunities or new ways to solve old problems. So, set a goal to start reading books. Twenty per year may be a bit ambitious, but you could read one a month or even six per year. Reading books also allows you to recommend books to others or share books as gifts, thus implementing the ever-so-important concept of adding value.

Adding value is about fully understanding the business issue and how it affects revenue, expenses, and risk. It is being able to relate to their business issues beyond product features and benefits. It is understanding their business and how what you offer not only impacts them, but their customers. Adding value is having a broader discussion that goes beyond just the immediate issue. As the sales rep, you are seeking to be an asset, bring innovation, teach something new, and help them achieve their goals. When you do that, the customer will buy from you!

Being a good listener adds value. People want to feel heard. Learn to listen. When I ask people if they are good listeners, I get a mixed response. When asked if they can improve, everyone says "yes." But when asked how many books they have read, or CDs they have listened to, or courses they have taken on effective listening, the answer is typically "none." Being a good listener says to the other person that you value them and are interested in what they have to say. To be a good listener, you must first know *how* to be a good listener, desire to be a good listener, and then practice being a good listener. Without conscious practice, you will not succeed.

Some practical steps on developing good listening skills:

- Be fully present – your attention is focused on them.
- Face the speaker, maintain eye contact, and have good posture.
- Pause before you speak, and remember to breathe.
- Listen without having an answer. Be intent on understanding them, not just waiting for you to talk.

- Take notes. This keeps you focused on what they are saying and helps with meeting summaries.
- Paraphrase back what they said. This shows that you have heard them. It also gives them an opportunity to share more information, which they generally will.
- Ask questions. This is more important than just saying, "That's interesting, tell me more," or, "What was the cause?" or, "What will that do for you?" Ask "what, where, when, and how questions.
- Summarize what was said before moving on to the next topic or giving your answer. This demonstrates that you heard them and that they are finished explaining.

Know that people want to be heard before they can hear you. As Steven Covey states in his book, *The Seven Habits of Highly Effective People,* "Seek to understand before you try to be understood." When someone knows you have heard them, you establish trust.

Practice listening skills with your peers at work or with your family. You will be surprised how much it will build trust, resolve minor problems, and create a much happier environment. Many problems in marriage and family, especially with a parent-teenager relationship, are related to the fact that neither party is truly listening; teenagers just want to be heard. You must first truly hear before the other person can hear you!

Other ways to add value:

- Recommend a book you have read.
- Give them a book you have read. Use sticky notes to highlight important pages, and put a personal, hand-written note in it. Clients love this!
- Send an article related to their business issues or personal issues. Snail mail (US Mail) and fax work well. People rarely

get personal mail or faxes, so curiosity causes them to open it. Write a personal note on the fax or article mailed.

- Blog on industry topics or on leadership.
- Network them with someone of interest or a good business connection.
- Give yourself homework that the prospect agrees to, and then complete the homework in the time frame agreed upon. I do this with networking my prospects with someone of value. When you complete your homework, you show that you have integrity.
- Send them a cartoon to lighten their day. It must be tactful and relevant to a situation both of you can relate to.

The above suggestions are to focus on building trust through personal engagements of value. The buyer will not only be looking for value that impacts him or her personally, but also for value for the company or for his/her team. The value-based sales rep will bring knowledge and ask questions that are relevant to their situation. The sales rep will apply the Seven Rules of the Customer listed in Chapter 7, talking in the language of the buyer; coordinating resources to provide the buyer the right information; offering options or new solutions that were not considered; being readily accessible; providing timely answers; and reducing the buyer's risk.

# Chapter 11

# Understanding Buying Criteria

Marketing departments are great at creating fancy brochures and websites with awesome graphics telling all the features and benefits of your products and services. The challenge is that so are all your competitors. In the 21st century, there is rarely a competitor who will admit that they can't meet your customer's needs. In this economy, they could not stay in business without the ability to meet your customer's needs. The question posed is then, "How do we differentiate our product or services from our competitors if both can meet our prospect's needs?" The answer comes in understanding what the prospect considers important and how they will determine what offering is better or best.

The buyer is looking for the company that can best help them achieve their goals. Buyers generally have specific ideas of how they will evaluate each offering, and the evidence they are looking for to validate the offering. If buyers are not sure how to evaluate the offering, then that is a great opportunity for a truly customer aligned sales rep to educate them and assist them in determining selection criteria.

## The rep who helps educate the prospect is generally the one who wins the business.

This methodology presented below is one of the critical strengths in winning business. Understanding the customer's buying criteria is the key differentiator to winning a deal. For instance, if a regional IT company is looking for a new accounting firm to handle SEC filings, state tax audits, and corporate taxes, they would create a list of requirements. They may also include that the accounting firm must have 10 years of working with IT organizations. Both accounting firms, firm A and firm B, meet those requirements. Any other accounting firm who does not meet these conditions will not make the short list. But once the short list is made, which firm does management select? From the seller's perspective, how do you, as accounting firm A, outshine accounting firm B?

| Needs | Accountant 1 | Accountant 2 | Desired outcome | Specific outcome criteria | Evidence to validate |
|---|---|---|---|---|---|
| Mid-size firm | x | x | | | |
| SEC filing experience | x | x | | | |
| State audit | x | x | | | |
| Tax | x | x | | | |
| 10+ yrs. IT industry experience | x | x | | | |

The answer is understanding what specific criteria the buyer will use to determine their selection. In other words, how will the IT company know which CPA firm is better if both can meet the company's needs? What the sales rep needs to be asking the prospect is:

- What are your specific outcomes that need to be accomplished?
- What are the specific criteria that the management team will use to determine the best choice?
- What evidence assures management they are making the best choice?

Sales reps need to focus on determining the buyer's decision criteria, which is tied to closing gaps, improving revenue, reducing expenses, or controlling risk.

To win the business, the accounting firm needs to:

1) Identify *why* the IT company is looking for a new accounting firm.

2) Know what the company's goals or problems are, and the obstacles or gaps in achieving those goals and solving those problems.

3) Understand or identify the evidence that management needs to see to make the best decision.

4) Identify where the accounting firm is in their buying process and align their efforts to directly address the specific criteria in that phase of the buying process.

| Needs | Accountant 1 | Accountant 2 | Desired outcome | Specific outcome criteria | Evidence to validate |
|---|---|---|---|---|---|
| Mid-sized firm | x | x | Wants to know partners | Partners are easily accessible | Cell phones given, have lunch 4x per year |
| SEC filing experience | x | x | Wants to go public in 3 years | Smooth successful IPO | Have coordinated with national CPA firms in past |
| State audit | x | x | Seeking outside investors | Looking for state tax incentives | Experience with other clients, testimonials |
| Tax | x | x | Setting up subsidiaries | Tax incentives, LLC expertise | Interview other clients |
| 10+ yrs. IT industry experience | x | x | Wanting to take advantage of IT development tax breaks | Demonstrate specific knowledge in this area | Interview other clients |

Other questions should be asked to uncover the personal buying motives of the management team. Does one member of the team have more influence on the decision than others? Do any of the members have a personal goal that accounting might negatively or positively impact? Who will the accountants be working with, and is pleasing the internal accounting department, considering any associated politics, important to any of the key decision-makers? Are there certain bonuses that will be impacted by the performance of the accounting firm?

The accounting firm that best identifies those specific issues and presents how they will help management accomplish their goals or close their gaps, should win the business. This is the process of understanding the prospect and aligning your offering with their desired outcomes; this is Customer Aligned Selling.

If neither accounting firm understands the decision criteria, nor presents specific evidence that helps management validate their decision, then either price becomes the differentiator or the IT company maintains the status quo.

# Chapter 12

# Know How Your Customer Thinks

Have you ever had a conversation with a client or employee about a topic and you felt that you were never communicating? That is very common, and the reason is simpler than you might imagine. This situation happens in client relations every day, and it may not be that the attorney, manager, or sales rep is incompetent or is not an effective communicator. The real issue is that there may be a thinking preference conflict or disconnection.

You say, "What?" That's right, a brain thinking preference disconnection. Ned Herrmann Ph.D., pioneer of brain research, was a physicist and a musician – now that's an odd combination. He was head of management education for GE in the 1970s and began to research what science was saying about the brain and the way people think. Using EEG, Ned discovered that our brains have four unique and distinctive thinking preferences in terms of how information is processed. His research has been validated by many others using surveys, PET scans, MRI, and EEGs. For more information on Ned Herrmann, visit Herrmann International online at www.herrmannsolutions.com.

The brain has four unique ways it processes different types of information: four interconnected, specialized processing modes that function together situationally and iteratively. Metaphorically,

Herrmann classified those unique processes into quadrants for easier discussion.

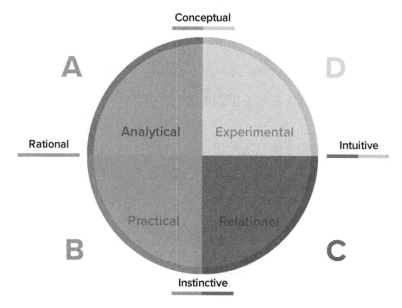

The four-color, four-quadrant graphic and Whole Brain® are registered trademarks of Herrmann Global, LLC. © 2016 Herrmann Global, LLC

Moving through the quadrants counter-clockwise, the upper left portion, A Quadrant, is referred to as the "rational self." It processes facts and data, does analysis, is logical and rational, quantifies, knows about money, and is realistic. The lower left quadrant, B Quadrant, is called the "safekeeping self" and is procedural, sequential, takes preventive action, is controlling, gets things done, is reliable, orderly or neat, and timely.

# Our Four Different Selves Model

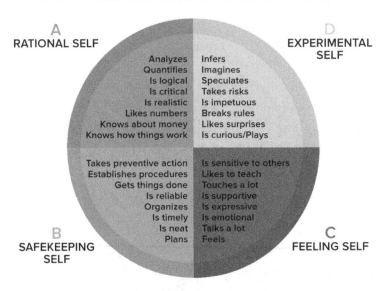

The four-color, four-quadrant graphic and Whole Brain® are registered
trademarks of Herrmann Global, LLC. © 2016 Herrmann Global, LLC

The lower right portion of the brain quadrant metaphor, C Quadrant, is the "feeling self" and is where thinking connects with people. It feels and is sensitive to others, likes to teach, is intuitive, supportive, emotional, and expressive. The upper right portion of the brain is the D Quadrant and is referred to as the "experimental self." It synthesizes information, integrates and sees the big picture, imagines, speculates, breaks rules, and wants to have fun.

Everyone uses these four thinking preferences differently based upon their genetics, environment, and upbringing. Some people use more of the upper mode, such as CEOs, research scientists, or entrepreneurs. Others, such as teachers, project managers, and administrative assistants use more of the lower mode. Lawyers tend to be more left mode thinkers, while sales reps, artists, and entrepreneurs prefer more right mode thinking.

A person's "dominance" is their preferred way of thinking. According to results from the Herrmann Brain Dominance Instrument*, 60%

of the population is double-dominant, 30% is triple-dominant, 7% is single-dominant, and 3% is quadruple dominant. For instance, the double-dominant may prefer to approach a situation looking at the big picture and connecting with people (quadrants D and C). A triple-dominant person may want facts and processes and need an interpersonal connection to make a decision (quadrants A, B and C).

Where communication challenges occur is when a person is thinking and communicating from a specific quadrant (preference) of the brain to a listener who is predominately thinking in another quadrant. The greatest challenges are when the quadrants are diagonal, such as someone thinking in the upper left (rational and facts) trying to communicate with someone thinking in the lower right (feelings and expression). The lower right wants to connect via feelings whereas the upper left wants to discuss things in a logical sequence with facts. The facts person sees the other as irrational and the feeling person sees the other as cold.

The same challenge is for the lower left-thinking person, who is detailed and safekeeping, trying to communicate with the upper right-thinking person, who enjoys risk and likes the big picture. The upper right brain thinking person is thinking to himself, "This person is killing me with the details; why don't they get to the point?" The lower left *is* getting to the point, but they have to deliver the point in a detailed, sequential process.

The illustrations below are from Herrmann International's *Start Thinking* course on Whole Brain˙ Thinking.

# The Whole Brain® Model

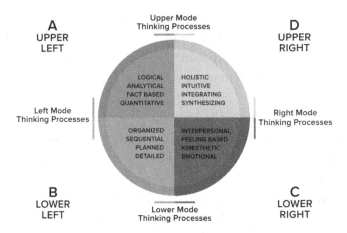

The four-color, four-quadrant graphic and Whole Brain® are registered
trademarks of Herrmann Global, LLC. © 2016 Herrmann Global, LLC

Thinking is FACTS, FORM, FEELINGS, and FUTURE. Another way to look at the quadrants is asking What, How, Who and Why?

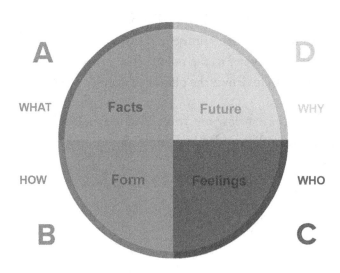

The four-color, four-quadrant graphic and Whole Brain® are registered
trademarks of Herrmann Global, LLC. © 2016 Herrmann Global, LLC

Another way to describe the brain's four thinking preferences is with four Ps, along with the questions a person would ask from that quadrant.

| Purpose | Possibilities |
|---|---|
| Where are we now? | Vision of the future? |
| What are our goals? | What are the key trends? |
| What are our challenges? | What changes do we foresee? |
| **Process** | **People** |
| How do we get there? | Who needs to be involved, and in what? |
| What processes do we need? | Who else do we need? |
| What are we accountable for? | What about customers and key stakeholders? |

In sales, if you have a technical sales rep who gives lots of details and is very sequential communicating with a CEO or manager who is a big picture thinker, there could be difficulties in that communication. The manager wants to get to the point and the sales rep is thinking, "I am getting to the point with these next 10 slides."

Typically, though, sales reps are more right brain thinkers dealing in concepts and connecting with people, while many operations people, CFOs, and COOs are left brain thinkers who deal in facts and procedures. There is great potential for miscommunication.

The good news is that people do not just prefer to use one preference or quadrant in their thinking. People use all four quadrants, but in varying degrees of preference or emphasis. In a few cases, some people may specifically avoid thinking in a quadrant; this can happen especially when someone is under stress.

I have worked with the senior vice president of a large food company whose job is to analyze data and develop the right product mix for each market. He is comfortable to be with, but is introverted. Under stress, he has a significant shift in his thinking process. He shifts to a very analytical mode looking for more data and wanting to process the information – a left brain function, or A quadrant. In the stress mode, he avoids communicating with others and is very quiet. He avoids engaging the lower right quadrant, the feeling/communication quadrant, or the C quadrant. A conflict will arise if the sales rep engages in the lower right (the feeling and people connecting quadrant), while not respecting the VP's need to analyze and failing to give him the facts or data to consider.

I also have worked with a manager who liked ideas, wanted to discuss problems, and was willing to try new things. A few months after my engagement with her company ended, I dropped by to say hello. She was not very talkative and was very focused on her work, which was unusual. Shortly after that, her team took the Herrmann Brain Dominance Instrument˚, and I saw her report. Under normal circumstances she is very task oriented, lower left brain. But under stress, she shifts to upper right brain - wanting to look at new ideas and new ways of approaching a problem. When I was working with her on a regular basis, it was a stressful time and she desired to look at new approaches. When I dropped by, things were normal, so she was operating out of her preferred mode, the lower left, which is more task oriented.

To ensure good communication, it is recommended that sales reps learn to talk and present in Whole Brain˚ mode: providing information and a discussion that engages all four quadrants. Once you find that a person prefers a certain quadrant, adapting to their thinking style will close more sales.

Recently, a CEO who is very fact-oriented, contacted me for sales training. I knew he was fact-oriented from working with him in a volunteer organization, and I also knew that he had a great deal of input in their website design. The website was very fact-based with few pictures and lots of organized data. The CEO included the vice president of sales in the discussions, and I immediately connected with him. Both of us are right brain thinkers.

After some discussion and agreement upon the goals, the CEO left developing the sales training plan up to the vice president of sales and me. We developed the plan over two sessions and did a review together before presenting it to the CEO. This review took about 20 minutes. When I presented the training proposal to the CEO, the review took 1.5 hours. I knew it would take longer because the CEO wanted to discuss every fact and the logic. I had designed the proposal outline with him in mind. We walked through each point while he took notes. After going through the entire process, he said, "This looks good; I approve it."

Since the vice president of sales had reviewed the proposal in 20 minutes, if I had become impatient with the CEO and tried to close the deal before he was ready, I would have lost. Also, since I knew he was details-oriented, I wrote a factual, detailed proposal with him in mind.

In a similar situation, I was working with a restaurant equipment company. After an initial training workshop, the business owners asked me what the next step was. I tried to discuss ideas and share what was needed from a right brain perspective. The two owners are very analytical and want data, what I was proposing did not make sense to them. To make it clear what I wanted to do and why, I developed a spread sheet showing sales quotas, activity levels, meetings needed, proposals given, and closes required to reach quota. I explained that each ratio had a specific behavior or skill that is needed to deliver the desired result, and I was proposing to teach those skills. Once they saw my proposal from a numerical perspective, they totally understood what and why I was proposing the training. They bought whole heartedly and it lead to a six-month retainer.

Sales people who consider how their audience thinks and then present in that fashion will sell more and sell faster. Communicating in a person's preferred mode builds rapport. Communication delays will be reduced, and trust will be built.

## Whole Brain® Selling can reduce the sales cycle by getting to the main decision criteria faster.

This grid shows how to adapt in a sales situation to each thinking preference.

### Whole Brain® Sales Walk-Around

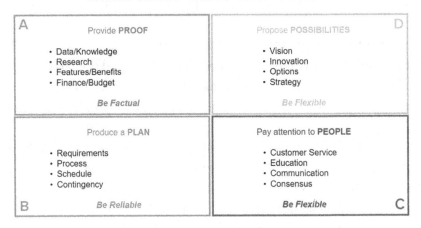

The four-color, four-quadrant graphic and Whole Brain® are registered trademarks of Herrmann Global, LLC. © 2016 Herrmann Global, LLC

I once profiled a sales team, their vice president, director, and eight sales managers. It was interesting to see how the group made decisions. Even though they were all very people oriented, their preferred quadrants were facts, processes, and ideas (A, B, D). The C quadrant was not as important, which meant they made communication with their team a low priority. Do you see potential problems with this team? After I profiled them, the Sr. VP recognized why one of their initiatives was six months behind. They had failed to communicate with users and the lower echelon of reps. The sales managers used the information they learned from each person's profile and from the team's profile with the

Herrmann Brain Dominance Instrument® to improve coaching their reps and writing proposals.

## Whole Brain® Thinking is effective in any situation from proposals to sales training.

Whole Brain® Thinking is not only a powerful tool in the sales discussion, it is useful in any setting from internal communication, strategic planning, and problem solving to designing web pages, trade show booths, proposals, standard response emails, and job descriptions.

Below is additional information from Herrmann International on how different quadrants prefer information to be presented.

## How to Present Information

| A | D |
|---|---|
| • Brief, precise, clear and technically accurate information<br>• Data and fact-based visual aids<br>• Well-articulated ideas presented in a logical format<br>• No assumptions<br>• Facts, not fluff<br>• Clear goals and objectives<br>• Answers to "What" questions | • Pig-picture overview<br>• Conceptual framework<br>• Metaphors and visuals<br>• Minimal details<br>• Flexibility to moe away from planned agenda<br>• Something new, fun, and imaginative<br>• Alignment with the long-term strategy<br>• Answers to "Why" questions |
| • Concise, step-by-step approach<br>• Consistency<br>• Punctuality<br>• Detailed action plan<br>• References<br>• Adherence to rules and procedures<br>• Something in writing, in advance<br>• Contingency plans<br>• No digressions<br>• Answers to "How" questions | • Empathy and consideration for others<br>• Eye-to-eye contact<br>• Personal touch and informality<br>• Open, informal discussion<br>• Expressive body language and voice<br>• Introductions and conversation<br>• Information on the effect on others<br>• Actively listen<br>• No hidden agendas<br>• Answers to "Who" questions |
| B | C |

The four-color, four-quadrant graphic and Whole Brain® are registered trademarks of Herrmann Global, LLC. © 2016 Herrmann Global, LLC

Here are other ways to use the Whole Brain® Thinking process in preparing for a meeting or presentation. Start with the D quadrant-what is the desired outcome or what is the future? Secondly, move to the A quadrant, presenting the facts of the situation. Third, move to the C quadrant, addressing who needs to be involved, the feelings of the situation, and other people-related issues. Fourth, move to the B quadrant - how or when your solution will be used. Too many times, operations people (typically left-brain thinkers) want to discuss how to proceed or get to all the details without considering the C quadrant of how people feel, or who needs to be involved in the decision or communication.

When emailing someone, try to create a Whole Brain* email. Use bullet points for the A quadrant. Use brief summary statements for the D quadrant. Give a detailed explanation for the B quadrant. And give a personal note to cover the C quadrant.

Here is a simple example of how understanding a person's thought preferences can be helpful. One of my clients sells to CFOs. His profile is more B, C, and D, and less A. CFOs are typically dominant in A, the facts quadrant. The sales rep was sending long emails with lots of description and getting no response. He changed his emails to bullet points and immediately started receiving responses. He even told me that one CFO would answer back in bullet points. Adapting to how your customer prefers to think builds trust and moves the sales process forward.

Use the Whole Brain* Model to map out your unique and distinct customers. I have used it to help my clients map out their customer's thinking preferences and customize their sales call toward those preferences. Oftentimes, your most difficult customer has thinking preferences totally opposite you, therefore you struggle to see things from their perspective.

One client sold very technical safety equipment to the public safety sector. The safety manager was the technical influencer, and the fire chief was the financial buyer. The safety manger was interested in the details and wanted to understand how to use it and the time required. His interest was in how much time the new equipment would save (details and process – think B quadrant), plus he knew that the firemen would have fewer complaints (C quadrant). The fire chief was most interested in costs and effectiveness versus the current process (A quadrant). They also were looking at how it would affect the overall safety processes within the department (D quadrant). Questions and presentations were designed with these two thinking processes in mind.

Another client was a physical therapy clinic. Sales reps had been tried, but had been unsuccessful in calling on physicians and nurses. We thought we would do something different (D quadrant thinking) and make a physical therapist a part-time sales rep. I profiled the physical therapist learning that she was very high B and C, and moderate D. She was a low preference in the A quadrant.

Her target referral sources were orthopedic physicians who are very strong in the A (facts) and D (big picture) quadrants. The office manager controlled access to the doctor, and she was typically moderate A, high B, and high C. The nurse scheduler was high B and high C.

We developed her sales call around those thinking preferences. Since she is a physical therapist, she approached the doctors from a clinical perspective, discussing facts about their clinic and the treatment plans. She asked the doctors what their biggest complaints in dealing with physical therapy clinics were. She found out that the doctors like to stay informed, so she started to personally deliver the patient report charts to the doctors, which they liked.

The office manager was concerned with the smooth running of the clinic and keeping staff and doctor productive and happy. The physical therapist/sales rep focused on setting appointments on a consistent basis and not just "popping in" to see the doctor.

As she worked with the nurse scheduler who is high B, the focus was to be pleasant and "not screw up her day" by interrupting her routine.

With these sales tactics in place, referrals doubled in 45 days and were up 150% in eight months. Two years out, total referrals were up 230%.

# 4 Quadrant Sales Meeting Planning

| What, Facts, Logic, Purpose | Why, Big Picture, Aesthetic, Innovative |
|---|---|
| • What is the purpose of the sales call?<br>• How will the customer measure success for this meeting?<br>• What are the customer's goals/needs?<br>• How will the customer measure Return on Investment?<br>• What type of account is this in profitability and maintenance potential from our perspective? | • What are their annual goals?<br>• Goals for this meeting?<br>• Do my materials look good? Am I presenting in a professional way?<br>• What are their long-term goals or vision?<br>• What type of innovation are they looking for?<br>• Am I flexible in my discussion |
| **How, Process, Risk Aversion, Details** | **Who, Feelings, Interpersonal Connection** |
| • Provide a meeting agenda<br>• Materials or information I need to provide?<br>• Am I well organized?<br>• Have I prepared for the meeting doing background research?<br>• Be on time<br>• Have references? | • Who am I calling on?<br>• What type of decision maker are they: financial, technical, user<br>• Who else may need to be involved?<br>• How to create an emotional connection?<br>• What are their thinking preferences? |

# 4 Quadrant Buying

List 4 things in each quadrant that your prospect may consider when evaluating your product or service offering

| What | Why |
|------|-----|
| • | • |
| • | • |
| • | • |
| • | |
| **How** | **Who** |
| • | • |
| • | • |
| • | • |

The Whole Brain˚ Thinking methodology is a very effective tool to establish trust, get to the key buying motives, and move the sales process along faster by aligning with the customer's thinking preferences.

If you are interested in learning more about how Whole Brain˚ Thinking and the Herrmann Brain Dominance Instrument˚ work, go to www.herrmannsolutions.com. You can also purchase the *Whole Brain Business Book* or download the four buying criteria mapped out into the Whole Brain˚ process from my website at www.billhartbizgrowth.com/wholebrainbuyingcriteria.

If you would like to see your own thinking preferences, contact me at bill@billhartbizgrowth.com to take the Herrmann Brain Dominance Instrument˚.

"A must read for everyone who wants to apply their whole selves in whatever they do."
—JIM KOUZES, COAUTHOR OF *THE LEADERSHIP CHALLENGE*

Unlocking the Power of Whole Brain Thinking in Organizations, Teams, and Individuals

The Whole Brain Business Book SECOND EDITION

Ned Herrmann and Ann Herrmann-Nehdi

You will get your personal report, a Whole Brain˚ workbook, and a one-on-one debrief.

# Chapter 13

# The Human Buying Behavior Model

## Human Buying Behavior

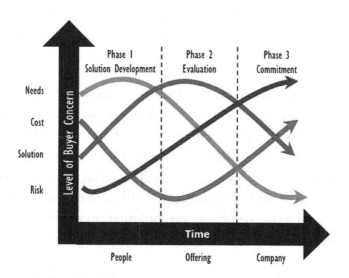

In a conversation with Neil Rackham in Atlanta at the Sales Management Association's annual conference in 2013, we discussed the complexities of buyer behavior and the Buyer Behavior Model described in Neil's book *Major Account Sales Strategy*. Neal gave me permission to further elaborate on it from my experience. For additional reading on this topic, read *Customer Centric Selling, Second Edition* by Michael Bosworth, John R. Holland, and Frank Visgatis. The authors also share their story of learning this from Neil Rackham, Ph.D., who developed this model from conducting 1,500 surveys of sales transactions while consulting with Xerox. With further research, he concluded that this model applies to any complex buying decision.

The time, complexity, and risk of the sale determine the time frame and progression from Phase 1 through Phase 3. I have used this model with multiple companies to conduct deal analysis. This model is very useful in assessing where your buyer is in the buying process, then working to align your sales efforts with what is most important to the buyer at that point. From that analysis, you then decide on what the next step is. Rick Keith, Central Region Sales Manager for Jack Henry & Associates, regarding teaching his team to use the buyer behavior model to assess their deal stages, stated "I believe your workshop helped my salespeople focus on completing each phase of the sales process before moving to the next. No question this helped us meet our annual goal." Rick's team exceeded their annual sales quota.

On the left side, the Y axis is level of buyer concern. There are four concerns during the buying process: Needs, Cost, Solution, and Risk. These concerns change in terms of priority during each phase of the buying cycle. It is imperative that a sales rep understands where the buyer is in the buying cycle because if the sales rep is out of alignment with the buyer, this misalignment increases risk, causes a delay, drives the buyer to get another opinion/quote, or brings price into the discussion at the wrong time.

There are three phases in the buying cycle: Solution Development, Evaluation, and Commitment. On the X axis called "Time," notice what is important in each stage.

On the Y axis "Level of Concern" during the Solution Development stage, the sales rep is the main focus. This is where the 39% in vendor criteria plays a strong role. The sales rep is the key factor in whether the buyer will move to the next stage or not. Sales competence in adding value is critical at this stage.

During the Evaluation Stage, emphasis is on the solution or offering. This is where the buyer will judge whether the offering meets their buying criteria, and will probably re-evaluate whether this is the best solution for their needs.

During the Commitment phase, the role of the company, its reputation, and quality are key in determining whether to buy or not.

<u>Solution Development</u>

The first Phase of the model is Solution Development. This is where the sales rep plays the greatest role, and has the greatest impact on the buyer's decision. The Sales Rep's competence in helping the prospect develop a solution is 39% of the decision criteria to buy.

In terms of concern, the need is forefront on the buyer's mind. The prospect or buyer has a need, a goal to achieve, or problem to solve. It is the sales rep's job to fully identify and quantify the need, its importance, business impact, stake holders, etc., while also identifying and understanding the relevance meeting the need will have on the success of the department or company. The more the rep can tie that solution to improving revenue, reducing expenses, or controlling risk, the better the opportunity is to make a sale.

The second important thing for the buyer is cost. What's the cost of the solution to satisfy the need? This is a value-based question. Does the value of the solution solve the need with an acceptable cost? For instance, does the value achieve return on investment, cost of capital goals, or fit within the budget? This point is critical to understand. The buyer will most likely see every solution as too expensive until key issues are identified and quantified, and value is established based upon their criteria:

1) The need is fully or clearly defined.
2) What is causing the need (problem or goal) is identified and its importance is determined.
3) The impact of the desired outcome, i.e. the tangible benefit, such as return on investment, return on capital, reduction of expenses, increased market share, improved customer service, etc.

Think about this: when you see something that piques your interest, what is the first thing you ask of the seller? "How much does it cost?" You do this everywhere, even when you look at the menu in a restaurant. You think, "What do I want to eat, or how hungry am I?", then "What am I willing to spend to satisfy that hunger?"

## The business issue, the impact of the need, and desired outcome must be fully identified and its value established before making a presentation.

By fully understanding this critical point – that the business need must be fully identified – the sales rep won't prematurely begin a conversation with a presentation or the benefits of the product or service. Instead the rep will engage in a business discussion related to specific issues he or she can solve. At this stage, it is important to discuss not only needs, but to identify the buyer's decision criteria - how they will know what the best solution is and what evidence they need to see to make a decision.

As the rep engages in a business discussion, a potential solution is being developed, i.e. the value. Depending on the product or service, this may take one sales call or more. The first hurdle the rep must overcome is cost. The value of the solution must exceed the cost, i.e. the buyer must clearly see that the solution will provide enough benefit/ value to overcome the cost issue. This is a value judgment in the buyer's mind. During this stage, the seller can fall into what I call the **cost cap**.

The prospect/buyer asks for a proposal, and the seller thinks that he or she has a hot prospect. In reality, the prospect is asking to understand or identify the cost. Many hours have been wasted on developing a proposal when a desired outcome and its tangible impact have not been identified; that is what will happen when this problem is solved or this goal is achieved, and what the value of the solution is. The seller submits a proposal and is immediately shot down with the words, "Your price is too high." Not enough value has been established in the prospect's eyes. If the outcome does not outweigh the cost, the deal is dead.

Understanding this point about the buyer's mindset is very helpful. It tells the sales rep to bring up a cost range early to establish a value, and if the solution is appropriate for the prospect. I do this often. When I have identified with a need and desired outcomes, I then discuss the value that my consulting or training would deliver, which establishes the return on investment. I share examples of results other clients have received.

Following that value, I give a range of what it will cost to achieve those results. For instance, once we have identified that the goal of a hitting the annual sales goal would give 3-4 times return on investment, I give a cost range for a workshop of $3,500-$6,000. A customized training course will cost $1,500-$3,300 per person. I don't give exact numbers, but a range to see if it is within their expectations. This prevents discussion on developing the exact solution, only to find out my fees are too high for the VP's budget.

Thanks to Mo Bunnell of Bunnell Ideal Group in Atlanta, I learned to use the question, "What are you looking to spend or invest?" instead of, "What are you expecting to spend, or what is your budget?" Posing the question in a broader term ("looking to spend") allows for discussion and does not lock your solution into their budget. It also lowers the chance of "price/sticker shock."

For example, "Mr. Prospect, as we discuss your goals and need to increase revenue, what specific sales goal do you have in mind?" He says, "I want to grow 10% this year." I reply, "May I ask why 10% is important? When you have achieved the 10% goal, what will that do you for you?" The prospect tells me that 10% will enable him to reach a new discount level with a supplier, thus increasing his net profit by 5%. I then ask, "Please share with me how that 5% increase in profit will affect you and your company?"

It is only when I get his root value motive that I can truly relate the value I offer to his goal. I say, "Thank you for sharing that goal. May I share with you some of the results my clients have achieved that relate to your goal?" I give the results first, then bring up costs. "To achieve these results, my clients invested between $1,500 -$3,000 per person. Would that 5% profit exceed those costs?"

Looking at the model, the concern of cost fades once a value is established that exceeds the cost. That is, a potential solution is identified that has enough value within the budget or one that provides a positive ROI. The focus is now on finding the exact solution to meet the need.

### Value Has Exceeded Cost

There is another trap a rep can fall into called the "solution gap." Seeing that the prospect is getting close to wanting the product or service, the sales rep makes the mistake of hearing the buyer giving "buy-in," or closing signs that the solution will work. They assume the buyer totally "gets it" and leaps or rushes to provide a proposal with the final price attached. The solution gap is when the rep has not fully identified the desired outcome, how that outcome will be measured, and the decision criteria. The prospect has not said, "This is what I want to buy," or, "Your solution meets my need or required ROI." The rep does not know the buyer's criteria for deciding to buy and, in many cases, how the buyer will evaluate the success of the purchase. Also, the rep may not have identified the small details that will give them a competitive edge, but instead is just providing a solution similar to every other competitor's.

## Jumping the Gap

The rep jumps the gap and asks to give a proposal when the buyer has not asked for a one. The buyer will use the proposal and price to vet whether there is truly a solution or not; that is, whether his buying criteria has been met. The sales rep made the mistake of being impatient and not confirming that the solution met the buyer's needs before writing a proposal. This is where price – a not cost – becomes an issue too early. Also, if the proposal is given too soon, it gives the buyer information to shop the offering and give other vendors the opportunity to get a strong foothold in the buyer's door.

Additionally, once a proposal is given, the buyer is pushed into Phase 2, the Evaluation phase. In this phase, the buyer thinks/assumes she has all the information needed and does not need to talk with the sales rep for a while, or any more at all, until a decision has been made. If pushed into the Evaluation stage without fully demonstrating that the solution delivers the desired outcome, the buyer may become stalled in their decision and do nothing, or they may search for another vendor who will offer more value.

## Are your sales people jumping the solution gap?

To avoid jumping the solution gap, use draft or trial proposals. These are email summaries that include a cost range. By using a draft proposal, you can once again engage in the need to solution discussion to make sure you understand the buyer's desired outcome and their criteria from which they will make their decision.

When presenting the solution, have the buyer's criteria clearly identified. Use the draft proposal, or meeting summary, to confirm what the buyer wants and if anyone else needs to be included in the decision-making process. A draft proposal can smoke out other decision makers before a final price is given. It also allows you to add products/services and adjust the final price. If you give a final price without fully meeting what the prospect wanted, you may end up reducing margin by having to add more product or services to close the deal.

Looking at the model, the issue of risk is very low during the Solution Development phase, but will greatly increase in the Evaluation and Commitment phases. Now is the time to identify and address risk issues. Identify them early so you can solve them before they become a great concern. If the prospect has an emotional response to risk, it is hard to reason with them using logic.

Thanks to the Internet, many buyers go through the Solution Development phase without ever talking to a sales rep. According to Forrester Research, most buyers are 57% or further into their buying decision before talking with a sales rep. The sales rep gets a call, and the buyer wants a price. That's it; no discussion, no meeting, just the price. When this happens, the buyer is near or in the Evaluation phase and is seeking a price to confirm the budget or value. If the buyer happens to still be in the Solution Development phase and just asks for a price without discussing their needs, they are in the Cost/Solution phase; they are trying to evaluate what it will cost them to solve their problem and the value of the solution. This is very typical of buying a car or even buying software. You can find all the information you need for Solution Development online. When a sales rep is engaged, it is very late in the buying process, either at the end of Evaluation or in the Commitment phase.

## Phase 2 - Evaluation

Once a solution is agreed upon, the buyer enters Phase 2 of Evaluation. This is where the Offering or proposal plays a major role. In the buyer's mind, Total Solution is the key decision criteria. Total Solution will be 22% of the buyer's decision.

In the Evaluation Phase, if you are the vendor who specified the solution, you are the lead, or "benchmark" vendor, as in Column 1 of the comparison. If this is a mainstream buyer, they may also solicit other proposals to confirm that what they are choosing is mainstream (Column 2 and 3 vendors). Based upon the other proposals, you may have to go back and further develop the solution, but you may move forward. Solution will be evaluated in Phase 2, with less emphasis on Needs. Risk increases at this phase, because at the end of the Evaluation phase, only one or two vendors will emerge.

# IT Data Center Example

| Vendor Requirements | Vendor 1 | Vendor 2 | Vendor 3 |
|---|---|---|---|
| Regional company | x | x | x |
| 3 or more data centers | x | x | |
| Designated account rep | x | x | x |
| Onsite support | x | x | x |
| Well capitalized | x | x | |

During the Solution phase, communication typically halts between buyer and seller. I call it the "black hole" of communication. The seller is dumbfounded that the buyer won't return his phone calls or emails when up to that point, they have been very responsive. The reason is the buyer believes that since they have the proposal, they have all that is needed at this time and do not see any value in talking with the sales rep. The sales rep needs to offer something of value to get communication going again.

The worst thing a rep can do during this phase is to call and just "check in," or call to see where the buyer is in making a decision. That type of call is very seller centric, not customer centric. It is all about the sales rep and adds no value to the customer. **All contact during this phase should be to add value and reduce risk**. The value may not be related to the proposal, such as connecting the prospect with someone in their industry, or even sending them an article of personal interest. It can be about things like a sports story or wine tasting. By adding value, either business or personal, you are communicating that you care about the prospect and are not solely focused on making the sale. Value = trust, and Phase 2 is a time to focus on continuing to build trust. More trust = less risk.

The risk increases as your prospect evaluates the offering. "What will happen when I commit and spend this money? Will I truly get the value I need? What is the opportunity cost of going with this solution or vendor?" Risk can kill a deal. Risk is emotional in nature and may be driven by or have a personal motive involved: power, approval, comfort or security. Since risk has an emotional component, which is in the C - *Feelings* quadrant just trying to lower risk by addressing facts (A Quadrant) or through processes (B-quadrant) misses connecting emotionally with the person and may not be enough to reduce their feelings of risk.

## Do not call just to "check in" on where the deal is.

To reduce the potential for conflict, address the emotional issue of risk before moving to the logical answer. You can do so by understanding their risk issues and restating them. You can also offer some emotional validation by practicing good listening skills. For example, you might say, "I understand that you are concerned with the time frame of the implementation and the negative consequences of a delay. That is a reasonable concern, and others in your position have had the same concern." Hopefully you identified these risks up front, and you then review the solutions included in the proposal to address those risks; talking with other clients who had similar proposals, a plant tour, pilot project, guarantees and/or penalties in the contract, or even meeting your executive team, for instance.

At the end of the Evaluation stage, Phase 2, the buyer's main concern is risk. They may once again raise concerns or possible objections to moving forward. If you as the vendor have made it this far, the good news is that you are probably the only one they are talking with. You are the Column 1, or the chosen party. The buyer is now evaluating the solution and the company once again. If an objection is raised, go back and review the solution and correlate outcomes to the proposal. DO NOT use "sales closing techniques" to handle objections. Using manipulative techniques that were made popular in the 1980s and 1990s just alienates the buyer. For instance, "I know how you feel, others have felt that way but found that…" There are way too many "closing techniques" to address, but most are manipulative. Manipulative techniques are negative reinforcing events and thus reduce trust. Remember for every R- experience, four R+ experiences are needed to bounce back. Build trust through valid questions and demonstrating value.

## Traditional closing techniques are manipulative and break trust.

DO NOT drop your price at this stage in an attempt to move the buyer forward to buy! If you do this, you just confirm the buyer's concerns that there could be more risk involved. This is what happens when many companies try to get buyers to commit to buy to meet a monthly or quarterly forecast. Using techniques to manipulate the buyer is what I call the "**risk gap.**" The sales rep has ignored the buyer's concerns and has jumped into Phase 3 – trying to close the deal – thus creating a risk gap. Risk must be overcome before price concessions are made! Lowering your price should not be a technique to get the buyer to go with the deal. It is manipulation, and the buyer knows it! You are also conditioning the buyer to wait until the last minute to get more price concessions. Computer Associates was notorious for using price to close a deal; their customers learned to wait until December to negotiate a much lower price. To reduce risk, go backwards on the chart and review the solution, and discuss if any needs or criteria have changed.

Do this quick review with all the decision makers to help reduce the concerns of risk.

Be aware that most buyers attempt to use a lower price to reduce risk because they don't see another obvious way to do so. Before you lower your price, be sure that it is the real issue. If risk is the real issue, the buyer is not ready to buy. If price is the *only* issue, then the buyer is in the Commitment phase and is negotiating to purchase. This is a key point! Too many times price has been dropped when the real issue was risk.

## Buyers attempt to lower risk through getting a lower price.

I explained this concept of the buyer trying to reduce risk with price to a sales manager who worked for a Caterpillar dealership; we'll call him Sam. Sam called me a week later and told me that the model worked. I quickly said, "Tell me more." One of his reps had an $800,000 deal stalled. The buyer kept saying the price was too high, but Sam would not allow the rep to lower the price. When I explained this concept of risk and price, Sam realized what the real issue was. The buyer used a cheaper bulldozer brand that broke down often, so he carried approximately $20,000 worth of parts in inventory. The buyer was concerned that by buying Caterpillar, he would have to purchase an additional $20,000 of Caterpillar parts inventory. Sam met with the buyer and offered him a one-year extension warranty on parts and service. The buyer loved it and inked the deal. Sam's comments were, "Offering a one-year additional warranty on parts and service was not a real cost to us. The brand he was using had major break downs within 2-3 years of service. Caterpillar will go 4-5 years before having any major service issues. I reduced his risk, and he bought."

If you feel the buyer is using price to reduce risk, then ask this question: "Mr. Buyer, outside of price, is our offering what you want to buy? What you are telling me is that there are no other issues, and you are negotiating a price with which you are going to purchase our products or services?" If the buyer says yes, then he really is in the Commitment phase and is trying to buy. If he says no, then ask to set price aside and talk about his concerns. "Mr. Buyer, may we set price aside, and address your other concerns regarding getting the outcomes you desire from using our product or service?"

## Phase 3 - Commitment

Once you have overcome the solution to the risk issue, the 3rd phase is where the Company's reputation and implementation is of the greatest importance, and is the focus of risk. Quality is part of the company's reputation, and 21% of vendor criteria is addressed in this phase. Price, not budgeted cost, has now re-entered the buyer's mind. The key word is "price:" what the buyer is realistically willing to pay. Price is important at this point, but to the buyer, it comprises only 18% of the buying decision. At this point, there may be negotiation related to price and terms. If the sales rep has shown value that delivers a sufficient return on investment or the desired outcome, price rarely comes into question. Once that is complemented, the buyer's focus is on implementation. If price is dropped, the sales rep should never offer a discount without getting something in return (refer back to the Evaluation phase).

The key point is that *risk never decreases*. As the customer (notice moving from buyer to customer) implements the solution with the vendor, there are implementation and usage concerns in his mind.

When a sales rep says that he lost a deal due to price, that objection is just what the buyer told them; however, in all probability, the deal was not solidified in Phase 1: Solution Development. The buyer did not see any differential value from one product offering to another, thus price was the only differentiator.

The rep may have been equating solution to need without fully identifying the value needed, or closing the solution gap. At that point, the rep probably offered a proposal with a price quote. The proposal gave the buyer enough information to shop the offering with other suppliers. These suppliers either low-balled the price to get the business or offered a better solution, hence outselling your own sales rep. The other vendor was more competent in understanding the buyer's needs and developing a feasible solution.

Another scenario is that the prospect never bought anything because he could not find a solution that fit his/her needs and justified the investment. If the deal was not lost to a poor solution, then it was probably lost to risk, and not to price. But be aware that buyers will try to use price to reduce risk.

Knowing that price is only 18% of a buyer's criteria, don't assume that when the buyer tells you, "Your price is too high," that it is. Start with a solution development review, through the quality of the offering, and the confidence the buyer has in your offering and company. If the buyer agrees to the criteria, then negotiate price, but not before. Most of the time, when the value of the solution, or the desired outcome is believed to be achievable by the buyer, he/she does not focus on the price issue. Price is then irrelevant, and the solution outweighs any reasonable price.

How to Negotiate

If the buyer is really trying to buy and requires a lower price, never lower it without getting something in return. If you cut your price without getting something back, you have just devalued your offering and are encouraging even more price reduction. The customer is thinking, "How much are you holding out if you just cut your price? Your offering is not that valuable after all."

There are three ways to negotiate:

1. Give something, such as a price reduction, to get the something of value from the customer.
2. Take away something of value to the customer when you reduce the price.
3. Hold your price the same and give more value.

Option 1- If you are willing to cut your price, require the customer to give you something in return. It could be that he signs today, or extends the contract two years, or increases the quantity of the order. You may negotiate that the customer personally introduces you to two other key decision makers in other departments. If you do that, be sure to put those terms in the agreement. If you negotiated it, then it is important enough to put into the agreement. The key is that the customer has to give something of value in return.

Option 2 - If you are going to lower your price, then either take something away or reduce an item in the offering. For instance, "Yes, Mr. Buyer, we can offer you a 10% discount, but that will reduce your service from 24x7 to 8-5 each day." Or reduce a feature in the offering, like the dealership did with me when I bought a car. "For that price, Mr. Hart, we cannot give you the deluxe model with both the leather seats and sunroof." If you are curious, my wife's car does not have a sunroof, but does have leather seats.

When negotiating, always give your most valuable offering or reduction first, i.e. your best effort. You want to show the buyer that you are negotiating in good faith. If you must do a price reduction and you are allowed 15% by your boss, give 10% first. If that does not work, then negotiate for something and give 3%, then 2%. The key is that you want to show a declining value every time the buyer asks for more discounts. Be sure to get something in return each time you discount. The buyer will wonder how deep the well is if you begin with your least valuable concession such as 2%, then 3%, then 10%. You may claim that is all you have, but does the buyer believe you? You did not show a declining value in negotiations. Instead, you showed there was more value if the buyer negotiated harder.

Option 3 – Give something of value, but hold your price, as with my example with Sam and the Caterpillar deal. He kept his price the same, but offered more value: extended warranty and service. One of my buyers asked me to spend more time with a sales manager during training. He did not feel there was enough time allocated to coach the sales manager, so I added eight hours of time without cutting my price.

A Sales Example

You are looking to buy a new flat screen TV for your conference room. In Phase 1, you do most of your research via the Internet, using Consumer Reports, Amazon.com, and other websites. Your desires – features, quality, remote control, Internet capability, etc. – are your concerns. You then form a budget.

You go to two big-box electronics stores to see the models you selected. Your experience with the sales rep will determine if you stay in the store and consider what they have to offer in terms of products, services, and price. If at store #1 the sales rep is knowledgeable and helpful in your discussion, you will see value. The rep may be effective in asking the right questions and offering good solutions: demonstrations, product knowledge, warranty, installation, training, phone support, etc. Thus, you will move through Phase 2 and Phase 3, and make your purchase right there. You will never go to big box store #2. If the quality and price were similar (you checked those online), the two determining factors are the sales rep's competence and the total solution (installation, warranty, etc.).

If the sales rep at store #1 says, "Call me if I can help," and leaves you alone, he has not added value. You might find what you are looking for, but you are prime "pickings" for the competitor to give you a better experience. You most likely will go to store #2 to see if what they offer is equal or better than big box store #1. If neither store has added value through the sales rep experience or total solution (i.e. the offering), you may observe and learn about the product and then buy it online.

Assuming both big box store #1 and #2 are equal in the sales rep's ability to help, you may evaluate what they offer in terms of installation, warranty, etc. Once you have evaluated those and determined which store to buy from, you are near Phase 3. When an offering is decided upon, risk increases as you near being ready to purchase. Before you buy, your risk is, "What if I made a bad decision? What if the store does not deliver like they said they would? What if I could find a better value online?" How well the sales rep handles your concerns will determine if you purchase the TV from that store.

Once your concerns are answered during the "I want to think about it" stage, you are now ready to purchase. At this point, you may do a little negotiating on price. You just found the same TV online for $100 less. How important $100 is in comparison to all the other factors – installation, service, local presence, etc. – will determine if you buy. Most likely, $100 is not that important, but it may be, so you negotiate hard.

## Questions for Deal Analysis

Download the deal analysis form at www.billhartbizgrowth.com/dealanalysis.

Use these questions to determine where your prospect is in their buying stages:

1.  Where are you in the deal Phase 1 –Solution Development, Phase 2 Evaluation, Phase 3 Commitment?
    a.  What evidence is the customer giving you to make this conclusion?
    b.  What does the customer say is the next step?
    c.  What do you think is the next step? Why?

Phase 1: Solution Development Stage

2.  How are decisions made? In what timeframe? When is the implementation needed?
    a.  Who are the decision makers?
        i.   technical:
        ii.  financial:
        iii. responsible for outcome:

3.  What evidence are they giving to show where they are in the buying process?

4.  What is the return on investment or other business driver, besides price, driving the purchase?
    a.  Has the customer told you that your solution will meet their need and discussed how it will meet the need?

5.  What are their decision criteria and what evidence do they need to see to decide which offering is best?
    a.  What evidence will they use to make a decision?

    b.  Have you talked with all the decision makers?

        i.  What are each person's decision criteria? Risk issues?

## Phase 2: Evaluation Phase

6.  Have they made such a decision in the past? Was it a successful decision? Will they use the same decision criteria to evaluate this offering?

7.  If not made decision, have you shared suggested decision criteria from other clients?

8.  How is the communication process going?
    a.  What does the customer say is the next step?
    b.  What are the customer's risk factors?
    c.  How are you addressing or minimizing their risk factors?
    d.  What value-added things have you done to continue to build trust and reduce risk?
    e.  Things I have done to help make a decision

        i.  Add-value
        ii.  Address risk – reduce the customer's risk in going with your company, point out the risk of not going with your offering
        iii.  Promote the competency of your company
        iv.  Make the buyer's job easier or more successful?

## Phase 3: Commitment – the company

9.  What signs does the customer give that they are moving forward?

10.  What risk issue are they trying to reduce?

11.  How are you addressing their risk issue?

12. Are they using a price reduction to reduce risk?

13. What can you do to reduce risk without reducing price?

14. What is the next step from the buyer's perspective?

15. What is the next step from your perspective?

16. What outside factors may have changed that affect the buyer's risk?

17. How can you emphasize the quality and history of your offering?
    a. How important is that issue to the buyer?

Price negotiations

18. What are you willing to give to get the business?
19. What is the client willing to give up to get your solution?
20. What is the top thing you are willing to negotiate with as your best offer up front?

# Chapter 14

# Being the Customer's Champion

Today's sales reps must be the customer's champion. As Howard Stevens states, companies want a sales rep to see things from their point of view. Being a customer's champion means that as a sales rep, you must have good relationships on both sides. You need to have relationships with the key players within your customer's organization, as well as your own. Too many times, sales reps spend time building relationships in the field, only to come back to the office and expect to find customer service, marketing, operations, or even HR jumping to serve them. A minority of sales reps understand that to truly serve their customers, they need to have well established and trusted relationships within their own organization. For there are times when a sales rep needs to ask for a favor or go outside of normal chain of command, and if there are no well-established internal relationships, that sales rep is relying on luck alone to get things done.

## Be the Good Stuff in the Middle

At sales meetings, I hand out Double Stuff Oreos and watch people enjoy them. At least half the group wants to know where the milk is! I enjoy seeing how people eat them. Some eat them whole; others will pull them apart and eat the crème first. After they have enjoyed their Oreos, I ask the question, "What makes an Oreo an Oreo?" The best answer I have received is, "It's the good stuff in the middle." That is exactly right.

Without the good stuff in the middle, you have two ordinary chocolate cookies. It's the cream that makes Oreos special.

Sales reps need to be the "goodness in the middle" when working with their customers. A good sales rep sees that he/she has two kinds of customers: internal and external. The good reps make sure they build and nurture the internal relationships so they can effectively build and develop the external relationships. The good sales reps are the "goodness" in the middle. And just like the two cookies, they are bringing the customer to their company and bringing their company to the customer.

Ask yourself these questions:

1) Would my customers see me, or my people, as the goodness or liaison in the middle? Or do they see us as a hindrance to getting answers or solving problems?
2) Do employees of my company look forward to my presence, or do they avoid me?
3) Does my presence make people feel better about themselves? Do I display a positive attitude and a "can-do" spirit?
4) If you are a manager, do you encourage your reps to build and nurture internal relationships? If so, how?
5) As a manager, do you budget money for building internal relationships with things such as lunches, bowling parties, or events with other departments?
6) Do you see the internal members of your company as your customer, or do you think they need to see you as their customer?

## Being the Good Stuff in Problem Solving

Being the good stuff is most valuable when you are dealing with a problem. First, you must realize that problems will happen. Unfortunately, problems are a normal course of doing business. If you do not have any problems with customers now, you will in the future. Someone in their organization, or your organization, will create a problem. Problems can be great opportunities to be the goodness in the middle and to differentiate yourself from your competitors.

An effective way to address a problem and to develop a workable solution is to use the Whole Brain˚ thinking process.

When you have a problem, start in the A-upper left quadrant - Facts: 1) What are the facts? What caused the problem? Is there anything else that contributed?

Then move to the lower right C quadrant – People/feelings: 2) Who is involved? Who needs to be involved? What needs to be communicated? What are the people feeling related to this problem?

From the C quadrant, move to the upper right D quadrant – Future or Possibilities 3) What is the desired solution, or what does the outcome need to look like?

And finally move to the lower left B quadrant – Form or process: 4) How do we get there? What process do we follow? What is the order, and what are the specific details?

## Problem-Solving

| 1. Facts/What | 3. Why and Desired Outcome |
|---|---|
| Define the Problem | |
| What are the facts? Cause? | What is the desired outcome? |
| Where is the situation now? | How will you define a |
| Where are those involved now? | successful future? |
| Where do they want to be? | Expectations for future? |
| What is the gap? | |
| How will they measure success? | |

| 4.  **How and Process** | 2.  **Who and Feelings** |
|---|---|
| How will you solve their problem? | Who are the decision makers? |
| Give the details of the plain | Who is affected by this problem? |
| Focus on reducing their risk | Are there any key influencers involved or who need to be notified? |
| Communication process is clearly defined and expectations are defined | Who do we need buy-in from for the solution? |
| | What feelings are present about the situation: anxiety, stress, fear? |
| | How do they feel about you or the process? |

Stress is caused when someone feels a loss of control and a lack of the necessary information to solve the problem. So, the first thing to do is to listen, and do it well. Have the person state their problem. Use the four quadrants method – what, why, who, how, and when – to get the necessary information. You must ensure that the problem is completely defined.

Second, restate the problem in your own words to be sure they know you understand their problem and the desired outcome. This step is very important before you attempt a solution. Restate the problem and then ask the person, "Did I clearly state your issues and concerns?" Then follow up with, "Is there anything else you feel needs to be addressed or that needs further clarification?" These questions are vital because they give the person opportunity to further clarify and affords them the sense of having some control over the situation. Once you have the problem identified and the desired outcome specified and agreed upon, then you can work on an action plan. Use the four quadrants to develop your plan of action.

Be aware that you cannot delegate the problem to someone else. Even if someone else within your company delivers the solution, the customer expects you to be the goodness in the middle, i.e. their agent back to your company. Be sure to communicate often, clearly, and thoroughly. Too many times communication is late or non-existent. Establish regular communication timeframes to update your customer, even if you have nothing to report. Remember that stress is caused by a feeling of not being in control and not having enough information.

If you promised to have a solution by 3:00 p.m. and it is now 2:00 p.m. and you know the problem won't be solved or project completed by 3:00, don't wait until 3:00 to tell the customer. Tell them as soon as you know the deadline won't be met. Telling them ahead of time may be unpleasant for you and them, but it gives the customer the opportunity to make adjustments. Having no information or unrealistic expectations creates more stress for the customer. In the event of a problem, keep the customer abreast of the situation and any changes.

Actions Steps

The next time you have a problem, address it in this order:

1. What are the facts and causes?
2. Who is involved and the feelings associated with the problem?
3. Does anyone else need to be involved?
4. What is the desired outcome from their perspective and how will you measure success?
5. Lastly, how will you approach solving it?

# Chapter 15

# Types of Decision Makers

Identifying the Type or Roles of Buyers

There are three types of buyers in the buying process: influencer/ user, technical, and financial buyer. There are also two personalities that can play a role: power broker and antagonist. One person can be in all three roles, but with larger organizations, there are typical two or three people fulfilling these roles.

An influencer/user is the person who has a lot of input into specifying the desired outcomes and what the product or service will do for them. This person is concerned with how the product or service will be used by their people and the final outcome. They are concerned about how it will impact their department or area of responsibility, or even how it impacts the mission of the organization. Influencers are people who have lots of trust capital in weighing in with their opinion on what is purchased and from whom it is purchased. They are typically motivated by a desired outcome or focused on preventing a bad outcome, i.e. minimizing risk of negative impact in their department or in general for the company. These people are not responsible for the financial aspect, so they are not motivated by the initial dollar outlay, although they may be concerned about how long-term expenses may negatively impact them.

The influencer can also be a power broker; they have great influence with many parties. Their input may be for their own career advancement (think personal motive) or it may be for other political reasons. If the power broker is on your side, that can be a great asset. In other cases, the power broker is not really so interested in the decision per se, but in how the decision is made. Their personal motives are to maintain influence or as much control in the process as possible. Typically, personal reasons are the motives for the power broker.

The technical buyer is the person who will specify the very details of the purchase. In terms of thinking preferences, this person is going to be more focused on the facts (A quadrant) and implementation (B quadrant) issues: what and how questions. If it is software, they are looking at the technical issues, number of releases, end-user support and other specifications. An example would be the IT manager specifying new software or hardware and then submitting the proposal for approval. The controller would be focused on the ease of use of financial software and how well other software integrates with the new accounting package.

Other technical buyers may be focused on implementation of the solution. This could be the Human Resource manager working to coordinate a training plan that the vice president wants for his all his locations. The HR manager must consider such things as cost of travel, venue, time out of the field, vacations, etc., and can nix a potential training vendor based upon these criteria.

One of my clients sells to the public safety and industrial industry. The safety manager is the technical buyer. He/she can specify exactly what they want, but the process either has to go out for bid or be approved by a senior level executive. If the safety manager prefers one solution over another, he/she will voice their opinion and use their influence to persuade the financial buyer to select their recommendations.

Typically, technical buyers have the power to disqualify a vendor, but not give final approval. Many sales training books teach that a sales rep should bypass the technical buyer and go straight to the financial buyer, then get delegated down to the technical for specifying the project or product. That recommendation works in many cases, but not in all. When I was selling IT equipment and services, one of my clients was a large insurance company. The CIO and IT Director had placed great faith in their departmental managers (the technical buyers) and required IT sales reps to go first to the departmental manager before they could go to the higher-level department executives. If a sales rep tried to circumvent that protocol and take their proposal straight to the IT Director or CIO, they would just send the sales rep right back to the department manager. Of course, the department manager did not appreciate that, so the chance of winning the deal just dramatically dropped.

With banking software or healthcare software, many banks and hospitals hire outside consultants to advise them on specifying the features and functionality they require. These consultants become the technical buyer. They are hired to give an unbiased opinion, but from what my software clients tell me, they already have a bias toward one solution over another. This bias may show that they had a positive experience with the software either through a former sales rep or in implementation. Many times, consultants also play the role of power broker, keeping sales reps from being able to directly interact with the end-user/influencer or even talking to the financial buyer.

In a complex sale, it is very important to identify who the technical buyer is, find out what their decision criteria is, and what evidence they need to see to complete their report and make a recommendation.

The financial buyer is the decision maker that everyone wants to get in front of. This person or committee is the one who has the pen to make the magic happen; they can approve the deal. Unfortunately, the larger and more complex the deal, the less likely this will be one person. As mentioned, committees tend to be the financial buyer. With banks, it is the board of directors. In other organizations, it is the department head, vice president, or a senior level executive. Most likely, this person will evaluate the proposal from the A and D brain quadrants, looking at the big picture and how the project will financially impact the department or company overall. This person relies heavily on the recommendations of the technical buyer and the influencer or users. He or she will evaluate the proposal from a return on investment, cost of capital, or other financial measure, plus the longer-term impact the purchase will have on expenses or future growth.

Understanding their decision criteria is key to winning the business. Ask a lot of questions regarding the project's overall financial goals or budget impact. The sales rep needs to ask questions from a financial perspective and from a futuristic perspective. How does your offering impact what happens next quarter, next year, or even two years out?

The last type of buyer is the antagonist. This person is against what you offer. This may be the technical, user, or financial buyer. In reality, they may be against all offerings, for they want to maintain the status quo. The reason may be fear of change or because your solution disrupts the current political power structure within an organization. Some antagonists like to disrupt just to keep people at bay; it is a power play. Antagonists typically have a personal motive in trying to block change. The best strategy to outmaneuver the antagonist is to get the influencer, power broker, or financial buyer on your side (as long as they are not the antagonist).

I had an experience with an antagonist was when I was selling IT services to a large gas utility. They were rolling out new client server technology to all their branches and did not fully know how to support it with internal staff. The CIO wanted to keep moving forward with change, using outside service companies to do the implementation. One of the area directors over the wide area network and servers felt threatened with the change. It appeared that she felt an outside company might show her and her staff up. She tried to block my company getting involved with troubleshooting problems or strategizing for the new technology. Her staff would not cooperate with my team, and when something went wrong, always pointed the finger at my network engineer. Fortunately, my client was the CIO and I had great support from the technical buyer, the IT Director. Whenever her people stalled my staff from getting their project done, I could appeal to the IT Director or directly to the CIO who was the financial buyer. Eventually, with much persuasion and leverage from the CIO, she stopped fighting us and started cooperating.

Action Steps

In your next sales opportunity, determine who are the different buyers and what their buying criteria is. If you are faced with an antagonist, there may be a personal motive that is keeping them from being cooperative. Work to find their personal buying motive and seek to win them over. Otherwise, align yourself with the power broker to overcome the antagonist.

Identifying the buying criteria of each role enables you to include key points in your presentations and proposals and leave out unnecessary information that will just create distracting "fluff."

| Buyer | Decision Criteria | Evidence Need to See | Role |
|-----------|-------------------|----------------------|------|
| Technical |                   |                      |      |
| User      |                   |                      |      |
| Financial |                   |                      |      |

# Example: Buying a CRM

| Buyer | Decision Criteria | Evidence Need to See | Role |
|---|---|---|---|
| Technical – Sales Ops Director | Interface with existing customer database | Working in 3 different similar environments | Antagonist – likes current system |
| User – VP Sales | Ease of Use | Testimonials and buy-in | Power broker |
| Financial – CFO | Cost, company reputation, connection into accounting software | ROI in 3 years, Tiered pricing Similar company using same accounting system | |

# Chapter 16

# Dealing with a Complex Sale

## Multiple Decision-Makers

In many buying situations, there is more than one decision-maker. In today's market, the larger the company and the larger the dollar amount, the more likely the decision will be made by a committee. Managers have less authority for buying than they did before 2008. Buying approval has moved up the chain of command where vice presidents, presidents, and even boards of directors are involved in the buying decision.

The challenge with this type of sale is that, in many cases, the sales rep only has access to one decision-maker who will take your proposal to the committee. As mentioned, many banks now hire a consultant to select the software vendor or outsourcing partner and then present their recommendations to the bank president or board of directors. The sales rep never has access to the final decision-makers although the extraordinary sales rep finds out who the decision maker is and gets to see them).

So, the question is, "How do you handle a complex sale that has multiple decision-makers, especially one where you don't have access to all the decision-makers?"

There is no magic bullet to this question, but there are certain

142

questions that can be answered to help you work through the maze of a complex sale. Seek help from your contact who is coordinating the information gathering or spearheading the buying process.

First, identify who all the buyers are and what type of buyer they are and their personal or departmental buying criteria. Are they financial, technical, influencer, or antagonist? Is one a power broker who can sway others – positively or negatively? Identify, where possible, any personal motives, for they are the politics of the buying process. If you have a person who is championing your solution, ask to have a meeting and discuss the personal buying motives of each person: power, approval, comfort or security. Also, discuss how they prefer to think and make decisions. For instance, if you have a committee heavily weighted with financial people, the A-quadrant decision criteria of facts and ROI will be very important. If you have someone from the users or Human Resources involved in the decision, they will tend to ask questions or have criteria from the C-quadrant determining how the offering will impact the staff.

Second, if you can, determine in which stage of the buying process each buyer is. Is the influencer ready to commit, but the financial buyer is still in the evaluation phase because he wants to weigh other options? Is the antagonist trying to protect the status quo, potentially meaning that the antagonist is really in the solution development stage (1st stage of the buying process), not willing to really move forward in the decision process or in the commitment phase as sees too much risk to move forward?

Third, with a committee, risk is one of the biggest issues, so focus on eliminating risk.

Fourth, make sure your proposal is presented in a Whole Brain' fashion so that you cover all the thinking preferences. Lastly, identify, if possible, the antagonist, who is not in favor of your solution.

In dealing with committees, ask the point person what role or function each person has on the committee. Just knowing their job function can help with knowing how they will make a decision in terms of thinking preferences. People tend to gravitate into jobs that match their thinking preferences. The highly feeling thinker (C quadrant) will seek other's opinion and want to feel good about the purchase. They will want to talk with references. The highly process or detailed thinker (B quadrant) may also want references; this is to make sure your offering is a safe or proven decision. A highly intuitive or risk taking (D quadrant) person may be looking at the innovation or futuristic aspects of the decision: "Where will the company be in five years using this product or service?" A financial person, seeking facts and using logic (A quadrant) will be most concerned with a financial measurement and the logic of the decision.

## What People Buy

| ROI | Strategic Fit & Innovation |
|---|---|
| Proven Process & the Safe Choice | A Personal Connection |

If you are presenting to a committee, before you begin the presentation, ask permission to ask each member three things:

1) What their job function is?
2) What is their role on the committee – what is their biggest concern?
3) Ask them to clarify their role on the committee
4) How they will define success for the meeting?

Knowing the answer to those questions allows you to tailor your examples to their specific issues. Tailoring personalizes your presentation which may strongly differentiate you from a competitor who just presents without knowing each person's specific criteria.

How a person answers also may give you clues to how they think and make decisions.

Creating a matrix to fully lay out all the buyers and decision criteria can be very helpful in knowing where you are in the buying process and knowing how much favor you have with the decision makers. Not doing this can cost you a sale.

I had a client in the restaurant industry who was dealing with the technical decision maker on a very large sale for a chain restaurant. The technical decision maker, George, did not want to give access to the financial buyer, Scott. George wanted my client to special order a grill as a pilot project in one of the restaurants. Installation in a test kitchen was quite an ordeal setting up the grill and programming it. My client had some leverage in terms of telling George "No" unless he could meet with Scott. Instead, he acquiesced to all George's requests without negotiating access to Scott or getting Scott's decision criteria. When the pilot project was conducted, Scott said "No" to the purchase of new grills. Because there was no discussion with Scott, nor understanding of his decision criteria, my client had no influence or leverage to align with the buyer and win the decision.

If my client had completed the chart buying criteria chart, then he would have realized that he did not have enough information on the buying process and used his leverage to get more information before setting up the pilot test.

| Mapping out the Decision Makers for a Complex Sale | | | | |
|---|---|---|---|---|
| | **Decision Maker**<br>Type of Buyer - Technical, Influencer/User, Financial | | | |
| **Features or Requirements of Product or Solution** | **Desired Outcome from Feature** | **Feature's Level of Importance** | **How Do They Measure Success?** | **Evidence Need to See** | **Personal Motive** |
| | | | | | |
| | | | | | |
| | | | | | |
| | **Decision Maker**<br>Type of Buyer - Technical, Influencer/User, Financial | | | |
| **Features or Requirements of Product or Solution** | **Desired Outcome from Feature** | **Feature's Level of Importance** | **How Do They Measure Success?** | **Evidence Need to See** | **Personal Motive** |
| | | | | | |
| | | | | | |
| | | | | | |

## Selection of Medical Billing Service using their software

| Mapping out the Decision Makers for a Complex Sale | | | | | |
|---|---|---|---|---|---|
| **Decision Maker – James Canyon – Financial buyer, CFO** | | | | | |
| **Type of Buyer - Technical, Influencer/User, Financial** | | | | | |
| **Features or Requirements of Product or Solution** | **Desired Outcome from Feature** | **Feature's Level of Importance** | **How Do They Measure Success?** | **Evidence Need to See** | **Personal Motive** |
| Insurance is billed with 24 hours | Effective cash management, reduction in banking fees | High | Improvement from current system by .5 days | Contract guarantees, talk with other customers | Performance bonus for reduction in expenses |
| Re-submittals less than 5% | More cash collected, less lost revenue | | Less than 5% | Data from Billing company | Less stress managing cash |
| Fees based upon volume | Adjust with busy season, | Medium | 3% expense reduction during peak times | Contract terms | |
| **Decision Maker – Medical Office manager - User** | | | | | |
| **Type of Buyer - Technical, Influencer/User, Financial** | | | | | |
| **Features or Requirements of Product or Solution** | **Desired Outcome from Feature** | **Feature's Level of Importance** | **How Do They Measure Success?** | **Evidence Need to See** | **Personal Motive** |
| Ease of use | No complaints from staff | High | Staff response during training | | Keeping staff happy, positive work environment, less stress |
| Tablet based | Doctors enter the data | High | Doctor's quick adoption | Doctors smiling | |

# Chapter 17

# How to Make an Effective Sales Call

Since I just talked about the new sales equation, I want to give a brief overview of how to make an effective sales call focusing on adding value. The rest of the book will give the finite details of working the prospective buyer or your customer during and the after the sales call to understand how, when, and why they buy. We will cover the buyer's mindset and his buying process, but before going into that, let's start with the fundamentals of a good sales call.

There are three stages to a sales call. An effective sales rep must master all three to be a value provider. The stages are:

1.  Pre-call preparation
2.  The sales call
    a)  Introduction and beginning of meeting
    b)  Discussion

3.  Post meeting follow-up

## The Pre-call

The pre-call is very important in preparation for the meeting. Do you know anything about the prospect? Do you know about the industry and what the key business issues are? Do you know what is going on with the company, its customers, and its industry? The

Internet is a wonderful way to glean this information. You should Google the company, the person, and even the prospect's customers (if known). Finding key industry trends and any government regulation that might affect them is beneficial. Use websites like LinkedIn and Connect.Data.com to find out who they know, work with, and any mutual connections.

If you know people who know your prospect, then see if they can give you insight on how the prospect thinks and what drives them. You are looking for information to help you better understand the prospect, their values, and how to serve them.

Other helpful discussion tools:

- Develop a list of the top 10 industry issues and bring them up in the meeting.
- Develop a list of issues about vendor selection and discuss. This will help you uncover their decision criteria.
- Develop a list of best practices you have gleaned from your clients to share during the meeting.
- Identify a gift to bring. I generally bring an article, one of my favorite books, or even the book I wrote on personal leadership. Bringing a gift creates value in the mind of the prospect.
- Create a meeting agenda to cover. You may or may not follow it, but at least you are prepared.

## The Sales Meeting

As you begin the meeting, you want to demonstrate that your goal is not a transactional sales process, but to add value, learn, and possibly develop solutions that can help achieve a goal, solve a problem, or satisfy a need. A great way to start is to ask the prospect, "What would you like to accomplish during the meeting?" or, "How would you define or measure success for this meeting?" This question immediately shows that you are there to make sure you add value and focus on them, not you.

Here is how I do it: "Jack, it is a pleasure to meet you today. I know why I am here, and I have even developed an agenda. But to make sure this meeting addresses your goals and is valuable for you, would you mind sharing what you would like to accomplish during this meeting, or how you would define this meeting as being successful?"

An example of how effective this question can be is a meeting I had with a CEO named John. I was introduced by an existing client, and the CEO said that he wanted to meet with me. The client knew him well and gave me some background information on his problems and what he wanted to accomplish. I did my research and felt confident as I went into the meeting.

John began by saying, "Bill, tell me about your company and what you offer?" In context, he was asking me to make a short presentation. I replied "John, I would be glad to, but first, may I ask you what you want to accomplish during this meeting? What would make this meeting successful for you?" John jumped right in and immediately began to talk about his issues. He talked 90% of the meeting. All I had to tell him was what I had done with clients in similar situations and share the results; I walked out of the meeting with a new client. His final words were, "Let's get started. Send me your contract as soon as possible."

### From the beginning, making the meeting about the prospect and not about you starts the relationship off on the right track.

One of the reasons I expected John to take control was clues from his office. In his office was a TV with CNN. The office was very aesthetically pleasing. He had unique items on his desk, including a mock grenade. He had a volley ball with a Sharpie drawing of a face on it. He walked in the office wearing shorts and flip flops. All this information was screaming D quadrant. People dominant in the D quadrant will want to direct the meeting and will jump from topic to topic. High D quadrant thinkers are also risk takers and like to make decisions and get moving.

As you begin your discussion, your goal is to get the prospect to identify a goal, a problem, or a need. To do so, instead of making a presentation, start by asking questions and practice good listening skills. If the prospect gives you a problem, ask more questions before you begin to offer a solution. I recommend asking at least three questions on a specific goal, need, or problem before you ever begin sharing how you have helped others in such a situation. For example, "If you solve this problem, what will the desired outcome do for you?" The follow-up question to their answer is, "Why is that important?" or, "How would that impact your larger objectives or your position?" You are trying to identify personal motives as well as business motives. Asking additional questions also opens opportunities to identify new possibilities.

During your discussion, your goal is to identify the decision-makers and their past buying decisions and criteria. Asking lots of questions versus telling what you do demonstrates that you listen well and enables the buyer to go deeper into their issues.

Here is a list of more questions you can ask to dig deeper into the prospects issues, most of which are courtesy of Mo Bunnell of Bunnell Idea Group. Learn to ask questions related to time, perspective, and connections: DIG questions.

*To download a copy of these questions, visit www. billhartbizgrowth.com/digquestions.*

Think in terms of four dimensions: future, past, elevate, or root cause.

## **Future**

- What goals are you trying to accomplish this year?
- What are you doing differently this year that you have not done in the past?
- Where are you in accomplishing your goals?
- What obstacles are you facing? What obstacles do you foresee in the future?
- How do current happenings affect the next six months?
- Is there anything different in 20XX from this year?
- Are changes in staffing, re-alignment of leadership, or leadership responsibilities needed?
- Why are those goals important?
- Are there any new markets or product offerings you will launch this year?
- Are there new partners or new market dynamics?
- How will business be done in the next five years?
- How do these goals affect your team or your department's future?

## **Past**

- What has not worked in the past?
- How did you get where you are today?
- Will what you did in the past work in the future? Why or why not? What are you going to change? How? Who will that involve?
- Have you been in this situation before? What did you do?
- Who was involved?
- What unique successes have you had in terms of opportunity or market timing?

## **Elevate**

- If you don't accomplish your goals, what needs to change?

- If you accomplish your goals this year, what does the future look like?
- What will change next year if you accomplish your goals?
- How will that impact your business?
- What impact will that have on sales? Operations? Your customers?
- How do you plan to integrate the changes into your current system?
- What new issues face your business? What opportunities or obstacles have these issues created?

## Root

- What do you think is the cause of this? Why did that happen?
- Who was leading at that time?
- Where did that problem begin?
- Who set the goal and why is it important to them?
- How was that process/strategy developed?
- Is there anything else? Anyone else?
- What were the parameters around that decision or success?
- Connections – who/what needs to be connected? Who/what is missing?
- Who needs to be involved, but isn't?
- What other companies could you benefit from?
- What facts are we avoiding or missing?
- What processes should we add?
- What people should be in the room?
- Who is involved in the decisions?
- Who is impacted by these decisions?
- Who else should know about what you are doing?

## Other Sample Questions

- Tell me more about _____.
- Would you elaborate on _____.

- Give me an example of _____.
- What else should I know about _____?
- How does _____ fit in the picture?
- Talk to me about your experience with _____.
- How do you handle _____?
- What makes this urgent?
- Why is this important right now?
- What bothers you the most?
- How tough a position does this put you in?
- How does this affect you?
- Why is this important to you?
- How does that sound?
- Do I have it right?
- "If you were to go ahead with _____, when would you _____?"

Use stories to share how your product or service benefits your clients. As mentioned earlier, stories engage the imagination, which engages much more of the brain than just talking. Sharing a story and asking if this relates to your customer is far more powerful than giving your opinion or telling them the answer. Stories help them envision achieving the same results as those in your story.

## By hearing stories, prospects identify with them and own the idea.

*"Those who tell the stories rule the world." -Plato*

Stories are the effective communicator's most powerful tool. To lead, sell, and communicate, you must engage and educate through the stories you tell. You must educate yourself on how to tell a story. Develop several stories from customer experiences. Write these stories down, and practice telling them. Practice out loud and record yourself or have someone else give you feedback on how effective you are at telling a story. A great book (and a short read) on how to improve communications by storytelling is *The Power of Storytelling* by Ty Bennett.

The types of stories you can share are:

- Client's success
- Overcoming challenges/obstacles
- About our people/individuals
- Future stories – "What could be"

The components of a story are:

- Beginning, middle, and end
- Setup – when and where
- Inciting action – what happened
- Build – situation gets better or worse
- Turning point – what happened, how you made a difference
- Resolution – take away, what changed

<u>Meeting Wrap-Up and Follow-Up</u>

Take notes during the sales call so that you can provide adequate meeting wrap-up. Summarize what was discussed, such as their goals, business issues, key metrics, and the possible or agreed upon next steps. I like to give myself homework that is of value to the prospect, and one that they agree to. For instance, I like to introduce prospects to my clients or other business connections. I recommend they meet my connection who could add value to their company. The prospect must agree that they would like to meet my connection. I also tell the prospect that I will send them a meeting summary via email.

By giving myself an assignment and delivering on that homework, I demonstrate that I have integrity and purpose to add value to that person's business.

> ***Make it your goal to be seen as a person of value, even before your business offering is seen as valuable.***

Here is how I prefer to write a meeting summary:

- Thank them for the meeting.
- Describe the current business situation.
- List goals stated, gaps, and causes.
- State where they want to be in the future and why – business impact.
- Provide possible solutions.
- List examples and outcomes of what I have done for other clients.
- Envision the next step. This could be something we agreed upon, or I may make a suggestion.

<u>Meeting Summary Example</u>

## **Business Issues**

- Your team is not producing at their full capacity.
  - o John is 80% of your company sales. He is holding his own but not generating much new business.
  - o Susie is converting 2 deals/mo. and has only been with your company for 2 months.
  - o Dean is at 3 deals/mo.
  - o Frank, being an independent contractor, brought 3 clients and has not delivered any more.
  - o Sharon wants to return as an account manager handling all the details of accounts.
    - This would enable the reps to spend more time selling and keep control of the details for each client.
    - Currently she is working on an hourly basis.

- You are considering a small commission plan for any new business she might bring in.
- Trish is the office manager and runs the VP Office program. She is a very detailed person and is not a problem solver.
- Sales need to grow and the team needs to be all on the same page in terms of sales tactics and verbiage on how to develop new business.
- You want a customer centric sales approach that focuses on understanding how people buy.
- You want some coaching to help you keep on track, i.e. be held accountable for your goals.

## Goals

- You want to convert from having to produce to keep the company going to more of a coaching role where you can manage 2 or more markets.
- Your goal for this year is to have everyone producing at quota of 3 deals per month.
- Be able to effectively manage and grow an additional market.
- Purchase another office after a successful year of management.
- Expand into other cities in the nearby states.

## Recommended Next Steps

- Implement a Customer Centric sales process.
- Coaching for you to learn how to coach sales reps.
- Coaching for you for your own goals.

Knowing that my email will probably get shared within the company and that people forget parts of the discussion, I also include a short summary of what I do, why I do it, client results, and, if we discussed it, a range of potential fees.

The other benefit of sending a meeting summary is that it gives you great notes to read over in preparation for the next meeting. The meeting summary is added to your CRM system via the email connection, and thus you will always have it. If the second meeting is delayed more than a month, I resend the meeting summary to my prospect right before the next meeting to remind him of what we discussed. For a sales manager, the meeting summary is a great way to see if your sales reps are truly listening and following a Customer Aligned sales process.

## Follow-Up Techniques That Build Trust

Since I know my prospect has many things going on and business people are forced to work on urgent things, I work to become a regular connection in my prospect's life. I work to create seven touches in 30 days so they are used to hearing from me and see me as a person of value.

Below is the schedule I try to follow:

- Next day: Meeting summary email; current situation, goals, problems, solutions, next steps.
- Within two days: Hand-written thank you note.
- One week: Email, fax, or mail them an article. Snail mail has great impact!
- Within 14 days: Deliver on something you promised in the meeting. This can be making a networking connection, or sending them a book, or answering a question related to your offering, etc.
- Three weeks: Email them an article.
- 25-30 days: Connect them with a referral or someone they could benefit from knowing. I try to personally introduce my prospect to my contact, thereby creating another touch point with both people.

According to research on predictive behavior, the follow-up has a much greater impact on the client relationship than the initial sales call. As much as 80% of a sales rep's activity should be on the post sales call follow-up activities. To change a person's perspective requires adding value over a period of time (see Chapter 5 on Operant Conditioning). Thus, the activity following a sales call validates a prospect's initial perception of you or invalidates it.

If you follow up and add value, then you have confirmed that you are someone of value, which creates trust. But if you offer little to no follow-up of value, then you confirm in the prospect's mind that you made a lot of promises but delivered on few.

Learning this concept from Axiom Salesforce Development, I developed a sales call worksheet to lead me through asking big picture questions, determining decision criteria, past decisions, and identifying who the decision makers are. This worksheet is a great tool to direct my question asking to acquire the necessary information to align with my customer's buying process. Typically, the sales rep who has the most information about their prospect's goals, buying criteria, and decision process wins the business.

When I share the client worksheet with people, they sometimes want to how I ask all those questions in one meeting! In practice, I don't ask *all* of the questions. I use the worksheet to guide my conversation and direct me to information that I might not have. I may use the same worksheet for several meetings to fill in the gaps to the answers that I don't have. The worksheet is used as a tool to find out about what is important to the buyer. Once you become good at asking questions, you will just naturally ask many of the questions on the sheet.

Most sales reps think they are good at asking questions, but when asked to role play a question-asking game, they show that their skills are not as strong as they presumed.

A great way to test your sales reps' skills is to engage in such a game. Pick a sales topic and have one person play the role of buyer and have the other play the role of seller. The seller begins the questioning. Each person can only answer a question with a relevant question. The idea is to move the conversation ahead without making any statements. I find that most people struggle to think of a follow-up question, but tend to start making statements the second or third round of questions. Another variation of this game is to have each person repeat the question they heard, pause, then ask another question. No statements are allowed. This game teaches listening skills, thinking skills, and reveals who is good at asking questions. Many reps claim they are good, but you, as the sales manager, know the truth.

A great way to learn to ask questions is to repeat what the person just said in a question format. For instance, if the prospect says, "I need to reduce waste by 5% this year," the seller responds with, "You need to reduce waste by 5%?" pauses, then asks the key question, "What is the cause of the current waste?" The buyer responds, "Our recycle process is using outdated equipment and we can't keep up with the current pace of material flow on the new manufacturing line." The seller replies, "Your recycle processes are old and you are not able to keep up with the flow on the new line?" He then pauses and asks, "Specifically, what needs to be replaced to keep up with the new flow?"

Repeating what the prospect says, then pausing demonstrates that you are listening and gives a person the time to think of another effective question. Another way to ask effective questions after a prospect has shared a need is to say, "Please tell me more." Using what, how, who, where and why questions enable a sales rep to talk less and listen more.

Action Steps

To learn to ask effective questions without stumbling, read out loud and practice asking the dig deeper questions on Future, Past, Elevate and Root and other sample questions.

Practice using the Client Worksheet in a role play. Learn to ask these questions by repeating them out loud.

# Client Worksheet

Date_____ Company _____

**Meeting objective Statement**

**Meeting prep**

1. Reviewed company website?
2. Done a Hoovers and Manta search?
3. Conducted a google search on the company?
4. Identified 3-4 key industry trends that could affect the company?
5. Checked LinkedIn?

**Your Value Proposition**

**Business Issues** (relate to profit, expenses, risk - people, data/knowledge, company stability)

1. Who are you meeting with?
2. Who do they report to?
3. Are they the decision maker? Financial ____ Technical ____ Influencer ____
4. What do they want from this meeting?
5. Vision – what big thing do they want to accomplish? BHAG?[10]
6. Strategy for Achieving the Vision?
7. What are their goals:
   a. 3-5 year?
   b. Annual?
   c. Short term?

8. How do they measure success of goal?

---

[10] BHAG stands for "Big Hairy Audacious Goal" as conceptualized in the book, *Built to Last: Successful Habits of Visionary Companies,* by Jim Collins and Jerry Porras.

9. How do other leaders or decision makers measure success of goal?
10. Specific plans to accomplish goals?
11. Known problems facing goal accomplishment?
12. External issues that are opportunities or threats?
13. What is the gap? Where they are to where they want to be? Why?
14. What are they currently doing to close the gap?
15. What are the negative consequences of not closing the gap? (This is a risk question that will help you in knowing how they will evaluate your offering.)
16. Who does the risk impact?
17. Is this issue serious enough to invest time, effort, or money to solve?
18. Are there other projects competing for the same resources?

## Past Decisions

19. Share with me your history of buying such products or services.
20. What goal were you trying to accomplish?
21. What decision criteria did you use to make the decision?
22. Did what you purchase meet your objectives?
23. What would you do differently in the future?

## Evaluating Your Offering

24. What is the client's decision-making process?
25. Who is involved in the decision-making process? Decision makers? Influencers? External and internal.
26. What criteria will they use to evaluate your offering?
27. How will they know this is the right offering – evidence? (Think of this in terms of a picture. Can I take a picture of the evidence? If not, then you need to dig deeper to get to the specific evidence level.)
28. What are they looking to spend? Budgeted? Non-budgeted? Range?

29. What value would the prospect need to see to cause them to spend more than their budget?
    a.  % more?
    b.  Impact of the value? How, where, who?
30. What would you be willing to sacrifice to receive a cheaper price? How much lower would the price need to be for you to sacrifice existing service or what you are desiring?
31. How do they evaluate price/cost?
    a.  Initial investment? Total Capital cost? Total Operational cost?
    b.  Impact on revenue? Reduction of Expenses?
    c.  Fits within budget? Monthly cash flow?
32. If talking with multiple companies or have other alternatives, how will the prospect determine which offering is <u>better or best</u>?
33. What do they need to **see** to know that one is better than another?
34. How will they evaluate their risk related to this decision: financial, achieving desired outcome, avoiding a negative impact? Relates to negative impact of not moving forward or moving forward and not getting what they needed.
35. How will they know that this offering will meet their needs?

## Implementing Offering

36. What are the steps that you take to make a decision?
37. When do you need to have this solution in place? (Do not ask "When do you need this proposal?")

# Whole Brain° Thinking Preferences

This person tends to talk from _____ _____ _____ _____ quadrants.

| | |
|---|---|
| A.   Facts/logic/reasoning | D.   Future, holistic, risk taker, innovative |
| B.   Detailed, controlling, risk avoidance, sequential | C.   Feeling, empathetic, concerning others/who |

# Chapter 18

# Management's Role and Challenges

Senior management plays a key role in how an organization sells. Typically, the emphasis for senior management is on what they can directly control – price, quality, and providing a total solution. Senior management typically leaves the role of sales strategy and tactics to the vice president of sales, or down the chain to the director of sales or sales managers, depending on the size of the company. To many senior executives, sales is a black wall over which one throws money hoping to get a good return. The sales process is viewed as an art, not a replicable, trackable, or scientific. Where many senior managers do get involved in the sales process, it is typically to help make a quarterly forecast. Pressure is applied to the sales organization typically in terms of increased activity: "Go out and make more calls and close more deals!" or "Drop the price to get the customer to buy in this quarter."

Setting a quarterly forecast based upon the company's need and using pressure tactics are typical and regularly made mistakes. Most older executives do not view sales as a science because much of sales training for the last 50 years is anecdotal or manipulative from the sales trainer's point of view, or is activity/productivity based to make the sales rep more productive. Little to no sales training or research is reported as far as what the client wants. You rarely, if ever, see an article in the business section of a newspaper talking about sales in relation to the customer. The Wall Street Journal and New York Times regularly report on how companies perform related to price cutting, quality, and even the solutions they provide. You will have to dig to find a decent article about how a customer aligned or customer focused sales process has caused a company's profits to soar, or the lack of Customer Aligned Selling has caused a company's profits to decline. Poor customer demand, poor sales, or the failure to grow revenue, is reported, but the cause of that failure (i.e. poor sales tactics in the field) is often not covered.

All these poor selling tactics mentioned, such as in the Barbara example, are focused on how the rep is comfortable in selling, or how the rep is trained to sell. Very few organizations specifically train to align sales with how the customer wants to buy. So where does the senior level manager's responsibility lay regarding sales training?

Ask these questions:

- Have you ever had a meeting on what your customers want from the sales reps?
- How often do you engage operations in your sales meetings, and discuss what the customer wants?
- Have you told your reps to cut price to close a deal? Did the price cut bring about an immediate sale? Or did the prospect still delay until another issue was solved?
- Do your managers meetings focus on sales activity and getting the forecast right, or do your managers discuss where the customer is in their buying process?
- Does your sales funnel in the CRM reflect sales rep activity or the customer's buying process?

## Managements Emphasis

According to Mark Donnolo, founder of The SalesGlobe, a sales consulting group in Atlanta (www.salesglobe.com.), the greatest emphasis of sales force change between 2010 and 2013 was in the area of compensation and quota setting. During those two years, in over

100 large companies that participated in his research, almost every vice president of sales was focused on addressing the issues of compensation and quota setting for the next year. Compensation plans are great drivers of behavior change. A good compensation plan can change the behavior of the sales force. But in most cases, the compensation plan is designed to make the supplier/vendor more profitable, and not the customer.

Compensation plans should be designed to drive profit and to increase customer retention and loyalty. The cost of losing a customer in today's market far exceeds the small margin or profitability gains made through new compensation plans.

The other area of focus has been on quota setting. Quota setting for most organizations is a number that is either driven by Wall Street, or by historical trends. Quota setting is not generally driven by customer needs and the customer's buying trends. It is done from the standpoint of "what *I* need" not what the customer needs.

Quotas unfortunately put pressure on customers to buy when they are not ready. Your customer does not care about your quota; they only care about their goals. Using price cutting to achieve a quota is manipulative and devalues your offering.

## Customers Don't Care About Your Quotas.

Training Trends

Training trends have been driven by several internal factors:

a) The sales process – from the seller's point of view.
b) The venue – time and costs.
c) A selection by mid-management with no tie to goals or specific results.

Most sales training is just product training. If sales skills are taught, they are about how to prospect, qualify, present, and close. The focus is on how to make the numbers, or the quota, in the time frame allocated for it, i.e. how to increase the personal productivity of a sales rep. What's missing with this type of training? How the customer wants to buy is what is missing! In many cases, the cost of training is more important than the results the training is supposed to deliver. Training is driven by a budget process, not a revenue-driven process. Few sales leaders ask, "What percentage increase in revenue will we achieve from this training, and how do we ensure the reps apply this training?" The venue or time frame allocated drives the type of training from a cost and implementation perspective. "We have a company meeting, so there needs to be ½ day of sales training." Or, "We cannot afford for the reps to be out of the field more than two days, so a seminar will have to work." If training is selected by mid-management, cost and venue are typically the key drivers, not application with measurement. Typically, senior management does not participate, and does not hold those down the line accountable for training participation or application. For those senior leaders who do participate in training, I say "Well done!" for you understand the importance and that the sales team is looking to you for buy-in.

My experience bears this out. In the spring of 2011, I was hired to do training for a west coast based company. I flew in and conducted training during a dinner session, and then conducted three sessions the next day. To increase retention and application, I gave the team homework from each session. As part of my engagement, I was to follow up with each rep with a one-hour coaching call. The vice president of sales and the national sales director were supposed to participate in the entire training. The VP participated in one hour of the total training, and continually left the room to solve problems. The Sales Director participated in about half of the training.

The challenge with this training is this: there is no accountability built in to ensure the reps are applying what they learned, and no key performance indicators to show they are applying the new skills. The good ones will take away a few good principles and attempt to apply them. How well they do is left up to intuition and guess work. The mediocre reps will revert to their old habits within 30 days unless measured.

Unfortunately, there are other challenges besides training. With my west coast client, the vice president of sales was challenged with opening international markets, and the national sales director was being called to solve problems due to production errors. their priorities were elsewhere. It would have been better to postpone the training until they could have participated fully.

The training was given to the sales team, but little attention has been given to ensure the reps applied what was taught. The homework given in the course was to help the reps retain the information and apply what was learned. To my knowledge, not one rep was held accountable to do the homework. The most important points to be applied were left to their interpretation, and I was not able to follow up with coaching, for all but two reps were "too busy." Interestingly, the two reps who participated in the coaching calls were the better performers.

In December of 2014, I was hired by a company that focuses on big box retailers to do three days of intensive training. The time of year and other constraints determined when and how the training was delivered. Knowing that three days of training is not very effective for behavior change and application, I convinced the owners to add seven months of weekly coaching.

The training event was very frustrating, for the participation was low – only 50% of the reps attended – and they did not pay attention. The owner would complain, but did nothing about it. The event seemed to be more about dinner and bar hopping than about learning new skills. I completed the training and began the weekly follow-up in January. The owner participated in two coaching events, after which he was always busy: on a plane, in a meeting, or something else was pressing. To the sales reps, it became quite evident that he was not participating, so they also decided not to participate. They showed up for the calls, but only one person was doing their exercises from the training class and most were non-compliant when asked performance and skills-related questions. After two more sessions like that, I called the owner and canceled the agreement. We discussed that since he was not involved, the reps were not buying into the learning or applying the things they were taught. He appreciated my concern and willingness to cancel the agreement. The sad thing is that he spent close to $26,000 on training and the travel costs, and got little in return. Without senior level commitment to learn the sales processes and to follow up with coaching, training has a quick, declining return.

Just as in golf, you can show and demonstrate to a person how to properly tee off and putt, but if they don't practice, the swing does not improve. Even with practice, the person needs feedback. If they miss the putt, the question of why they missed it typically is not answered. The same goes with sales. The sales rep lost the sale, but the truth of why they lost the sale is never known. The typical sales rep covers his tracks by saying, "Our price was too high."

## Knowledge Transfer vs. Training

The majority of "training" is targeted toward knowledge transfer, not toward behavior change. By that definition alone, if knowledge transfer is the goal, training is not happening. The class or seminar may be called "sales training," but, in reality, it is sales product or sales process education. Training only happens if there is practice and repetition. A one-time shot is not training.

Think of a sports team. The coaches may present a lot of white board plays and review a lot of films, but nothing happens until they practice on the field. Practice happens every day in sports, and feedback is given. Coaches ensure that practice is effective. They are judging whether players are effectively doing what they are taught. Coaches give regular feedback on how a player can be more effective. If a player was strictly judged by the score, a coach could not give him true advice on how to improve his or her performance.

Unfortunately, very few sales reps ever have a coach evaluating them in the field. Coaching is not telling the rep what to do. Coaching is effectively asking targeted questions to help the rep discover their problem and figure out their own solution. If a sales rep is told what to do, there is typically little lasting buy-in. But when a person discovers or decides for themselves the path to take and how that path relates to their success, there is strong buy-in. The goal of coaching is to empower people to grow and discover that they do know and figure out the correct actions to take. When, in the process of coaching, it becomes apparent that a rep does not know the answer, that is the opportunity to present a learning assignment. Have the rep read, review, or watch a video on the particular sales skill that needs to be learned. Hold the rep accountable for the learning assignment and test their knowledge or skill during the next meeting.

Two good books on coaching are *Coaching Sales Reps into Sales Champions: A Tactical Playbook for Managers and Executives* by Keith Rosen, and *The Coaching Habit: Say Less, Ask More & Change the Way You Lead Forever* by Michael Bungay Stanier.

Action Steps

Before your next sales training event, identify what results you want to see and what key performance indicators you will track to measure the rep's progress toward the results. Identify who needs to be involved from a management perspective and what role they will play in participating and any follow up. Identify how you will re-enforce what was learned.

A key question to ask is "Do my sales managers have the skills to coach the sales reps once this material is presented?" Most sales managers do not know how to coach. A learning exercise for your managers would be to have everyone read the Keith Rosen book and discuss a chapter each week.

# Chapter 19

# You Can't Manage Sales

In many organizations, there is a significant problem that greatly affects performance: sales managers try to manage what they truly cannot manage. They spend much of their time trying to manage a sales rep's outcome, i.e. the sales performance. But, a manager cannot manage or determine what the final sales results are. They can only influence the things a sales rep does to accomplish the results.

A football coach cannot manage the score; all he can do is manage what plays are called on the field and who plays in the game. The score will be determined by how well his team plays, the other team's performance, and the referees.

**A coach cannot manage the outcome. He can only manage the *input* that delivers the outcome.**

During a typical sales meeting, I have observed sales managers spending 60-90% of their one-on-one time with a rep reviewing historical performance. This review does nothing to improve the rep's performance. The last part of the meeting is spent telling the rep to keep working hard or to put more effort into the game and go close more sales, make more sales calls, or prospect better. The sales manager spends his "coaching" time telling the rep to increase activity or improve their attitude or get motivated. The problem is that the sales manager rarely truly coaches them or gives learning assignments to improve the rep's skills.

Here is a formula I learned from Axiom Sales Force Development:

Sales Activity x Proficiency = Sales Results

Sales managers can only improve a sales rep's performance by focusing on the input, the amount of activity, or the proficiency – how good they are at selling. In my observations and from what I have gleaned from other trainers, when a manager is supposed to be coaching, 80% of the coaching time is spent on activity, not on proficiency. The problem with that is if a sales rep is doing it wrong, then doing more of the wrong activity won't improve the situation or results.

The other issue is that most sales managers are great at identifying performance gaps, but are not proficient in the sales methodology to truly identify why there is a gap and in what skill set the rep needs to become more proficient. Again, most sales managers do not know how to instruct or coach the rep in that skill set, nor do they hold the rep accountable to learn those skills. The manager is not inspecting what he or she is expecting.

## Coaching – The New Sales Initiative for Results

Are your sales down in this tough economy? Many organizations spend their money on training the front-line sales reps hoping to improve results, and many have discovered that this is not the most effective use of their training dollars. Top performing sales organizations are finding the best bang for their training dollar in teaching their sales managers how to coach.

The Florida State University Sales Institute reports that coaching is one of the most effective sales force productivity initiatives. Unfortunately, coaching gets insufficient executive leadership support.

According to the Sales Leadership Forum, a sales think tank, 63% of organizations think their managers should spend 30% to 40% of their time coaching reps, but most (61%) spend less than 20% of their time coaching reps – about a 70% gap from where they should be. Do your sales managers fall into this gap?

Unfortunately, what most managers consider coaching is just focusing on the sales reps' low numbers and telling them to improve, then trying to motivate the sales rep to do so with encouragement or fear. Most managers coach in one of two ways: 1) telling the rep to work harder to close more deals, or 2) try to motivate the rep to improve their sales in a "Rah, rah, go team go!" session.

The 70% gap is there because managers don't know how to coach or what topics they should be coaching. Sales leaders need to understand that managers cannot manage sales results (sales results are outcomes), just the effort and proficiency. That is the fundamental flaw in sales management. Most of the focus is on the end result, historical data, and not on the effort and proficiency of getting those results! Just as in sports, a coach cannot manage the score, just the effort and plays run to create the score. The score is the outcome of the effort and proficiency of the players. If you are a manager who desires to be great, learn to be an expert in the sales process and evaluate your sales reps on efficiency and proficiency.

Jason Jordan and Michelle Vazzana write extensively on this subject in the book, *Cracking the Sales Management Code: The Secrets to Measuring and Managing Sales Performance.* This book is a must-read for sales managers wanting to effectively lead and coach a sales force.

Sales results are outcomes of a process and therefore can't be managed; they can only be measured. All a sales manager can influence or manage is effort and proficiency. Historically, most sales managers have focused on improving effort, not proficiency.

Take golf as an example. If I have a bad slice, more practice won't improve my swing. I need coaching on how to swing correctly and regular feedback from a qualified golf coach. Coaching has a great financial return. According to Ron Cox, CEO of Tailwind Consulting, most sales training is 25% effective at best. What is missing is the coaching component; the follow-up and continuous feedback. Ron reports that senior leaders who focused on developing others through coaching had a 27% performance improvement over their peers. Even more compelling is that executives who were the very best developers of other leaders were also 1.5 times more likely to exceed their financial goals. According to Dr. Brent Peterson, only 25% of the ROI from training comes from the actual training experience. A full 75% of the ROI comes from what is done before and after the actual training experience. Coaching is critical to getting ROI out of training.

As a sales leader, if you are focusing your efforts to improve sales strictly on sales training, you are missing a terrific opportunity to improve your ROI through coaching. The challenge is that your sales managers need to be trained on how to coach, and then evaluated to see if they are coaching effectively. The research says those organizations that make the effort get the results.

Zack Mills, former vice president of companion animal sales for Merial LTD, an animal pharmaceutical company, believes in coaching. During a dinner meeting, he told me that he decreased the number of sales reps that report to the sales managers. The sales managers went from overseeing 15-17 reps to coaching 10-12 reps. Sales went up because the sales managers could spend time in the field coaching their team instead of doing paperwork and picking up the pieces that many reps leave due to poor sales effectiveness. (Research shows that the optimum number of direct reports is five to seven people. That size sales team is the most effective for a sales manager to be coaching.)

Steve Young, former senior vice president of sales with Verizon Wireless (retired), began using coaching as a means for performance improvement while he was at WorldCom, before the acquisition by Verizon. To model coaching, he first hired a sales coach for himself, Renee Robertson. From there, Renee began coaching sales directors and sales managers how to coach their sales reps. According to Steve and Renee, sales performance and morale increased and had a positive impact throughout the sales department.

To learn coaching skills, I recommend not only reading, but listening to the audio version of *Coaching Sales Reps Into Sales Champions* by Keith Rosen.

<u>Tracking the Process and the Results</u>

The importance of tracking implementation of the training and coaching is given through the example of getting a lesson from a golf professional. The professional generally changes a person's swing. The person's golf game may get worse instead of better as he or she tries to implement what the golf pro taught them. She has not learned the new muscle memory and thus struggles. Typically, without monitoring the new way of doing things, or tracking the implementation, the person becomes discouraged and goes back to their old way of swinging. The new way would have eventually delivered much better results, but the person did not stick with it because it was uncomfortable and their results got worse in the short run.

Generally, there are no consequences for non-compliance in applying the new methodology or sales skills. Sales reps are not held accountable for learning, just the end results of selling. Senior management needs to regularly inspect what is expected, otherwise money is wasted on training and nothing is improved. This is where coaching plays such a key role.

As mentioned earlier, most companies track sales closed, but don't monitor the more exact details of how their reps are performing in the field - from prospecting to meeting with the decision maker. Few managers track "blocking and tackling," which gets you improved, or "yards-per-down," which leads to more first downs and touchdowns. A sales coach can help analyze where the performance needs to be improved. If a sales coach can make sales calls with the reps or observe the sales manager coaching his/her reps, he/she can then give immediate feedback. Immediate feedback has a much greater impact on performance than end-of-the-quarter feedback.

## Other Pitfalls with Training

Another challenge in providing training is that it is not designed for the different ways people learn. Some learn from lecture, while others are auditory or visual learners. Some people need to experience the process through role playing. Most of the time, training is designed around the venue or the presenter, not around people's learning style. Sequenced repetition delivers the most consistent results, but most training incorporates little or no repetition. In other words, using the name of an older sales book by David Sandler, *You Can't Teach a Kid to Ride a Bike at a Seminar*. A one-time seminar does not lead to long term change.

One of the greatest pitfalls of transforming a sales department into a Customer Aligned Selling process comes when a company's operations department is not involved in the transformation process. Traditionally, most training is focused on closing the sale; operations did not need to be involved. But, if the training is truly focused on the customer, then operations should be involved. This gives an opportunity for the sales team to discuss with operational managers where there are strengths and weaknesses in how the customer is served.

During sales training, many times I will uncover operational issues that are counterproductive to truly serving the customer. These non-customer-serving operational issues should be addressed as the sales reps adapt to a Customer Aligned Selling process. Operational managers generally see the situation from their perspective, not the customer's.

Exposing operational managers to Customer Aligned Selling will give them the customer's perspective.

World Class Sales Organizations

World class sales organizations are different in how they apply training. Senior management is involved from the beginning and stays involved, like Steve Young did at Verizon. The appropriate management levels participate in the training and coaching along with the sales reps. Management involvement gives credibility, motivation, and accountability. World class sales organizations see ongoing training as part of being successful, just as sports organizations see practice as part of the normal routine of a successful team. Winning teams are always looking for ways to improve. The training venue is designed to incorporate multiple training styles (Whole Brain˙ learning) and generally uses repetition to enforce learning. Effective training requires establishing clearly defined goals related to training and tracking the implementation through effective coaching. Lastly, effective training is focused on what the customer wants and how the customer buys, not on how the company wants to sell and achieve the quota. If an organization implements these methodologies in their training, they will meet their quotas, for the customer will be well served.

# Chapter 20

## Creating Accurate Forecasts

With the advent of Customer Relationship Management software (CRM), companies have tried to become sophisticated in their forecasting. Yet many a CFO still takes the forecast and multiplies it by a percentage of less than one. The CFO knows that sales people are overly optimistic or are concerned about their job, so they hide potential deals and load up the forecast with those unlikely to close.

I regularly see companies where the forecast for each rep begins with an opportunity discovered. The sales rep then enters a percentage of chance to close. As time goes by, or as a sales rep completes another process in the sales cycle, he or she generally increases the chance to close by 10-15%. (With many CRM systems, increasing the percentage of win rate is automatic based upon the steps in the seller's sales process, not the buyer's process.) That keeps the sales manager off his/her back. When the rep loses the deal, he/she claims that it was lost on price, or the buyer stayed with the current supplier and was getting quotes to justify the current relationship.

So much time and energy is wasted on pursuing deals that will never happen. Sales reps forecast opportunities long before they should. Many sales managers will tolerate poor forecasting by allowing the sales rep to make up a poor forecast with volume, i.e. having a lot of "opportunities" in the pipeline, and knowing that some will close. The sales manager then "scrubs" the forecast down to the sales rep's historical performance and submits that forecast.

Forecasting should be done based upon how companies buy, and not on how the sales rep thinks the deal will close. Forecasting should be done based upon the stage of the opportunity from the buyer's perspective. Evaluate the buyer based upon Neil Rackham's Human Buyer Behavior Model, not on the potential of the opportunity. The simple truth that reps don't like to face is that there is no potential deal until a buyer has told the seller that they have a solution that could work! Relating this concept back to the Human Buyer Behavior Model, this is the point where need meets solution. There is no true forecast until the buyer tells the seller, "I want to do business with you!"

Most CRM sales funnels are designed from the seller's perspective and not the buyer's buying process. By being seller focused, the seller records his or her activity and moves the deal on to the next phase, and the percentage win rate is increased. What you don't know from this perspective is what the buyer is thinking. Is the seller aligned with the buyer, or did they just offer a proposal? Is the buyer sharing a problem /need, the desired outcome, and the necessary decision criteria, or just asking for a price?

Also, within a CRM system, just because the seller is moving through the process, it does not mean that his confidence in winning the deal has increased. Most likely, multiple sellers are doing the same thing with the prospect. What determines whether there is a strong percentage of winning the deal is how well the seller is aligned with the buyer and how much information the seller has regarding the buying process, the buyer's criteria for a decision, and who the decision makers are. The sales funnel stages in a CRM should be tied to specific buyer stages and information the rep has obtained; specifically, the goal, problem or need, the value that goal represents to the customer, their decision criteria, and the people involved in the decision. When the rep has clearly identified criteria, and has interacted with the decision makers, that greatly increases the potential of winning the business versus the traditional way of answering needs requirements alone.

Looking at forecasting based upon the Buyer Behavior Model, too many sales reps jump the gap of matching needs to solution. They engage the buyer in a needs-based discussion, but when the buyer gets close to agreeing that the proposed solution will work, the sales reps gets excited, sees dollar signs, and offers or agrees to submit a proposal. While doing so, they are thinking or forecasting a 60% or greater potential to close. In reality, the buyer felt there was a potential solution, but was not totally clear on how that solution would work, so he or she asked for a proposal to vet or flush out the details of the offering. If the offering is what the buyer wanted, he/she will move forward. If not, he will most likely get another proposal from a different sales rep.

Kevin Davis makes this point in his book *Slow Down, Sell Faster*. The sales rep steps out of the mode of helping the prospect and into the mode of working to make a sale. He then enters a forecast based upon the seller's need to make a sale, and not where the buyer really is in the buying process. Basing forecasting on the rep's activity instead the buyer's activity skews the reality of a true opportunity.

## Forecasting should be based on the buyer's activity, not the seller's.

What the sales rep should have done before submitting the proposal is slow down, review all the details from needs to solution, and then get the buyer to agree that the offering can deliver the desired outcome.

Mo Bunnell, of Bunnell Idea Group in Atlanta, says, "A great way to ensure the solution meets the budget or cost expectations of the buyer is to ask, 'How much are you looking to spend?' during the earlier or mid stages of the needs to solution process." Notice the verbiage "looking," verses using the words "budgeted" or "planning." This is an emotional question that will help identify what the buyer is really wanting to spend and what their intentions are. Budgets cannot always be trusted; a buyer may spend more by robbing other budgets, or may spend less, using the budgeted money somewhere else.

The key to forecasting is to ensure that there is an alignment (Human Buyer Behavior Model – end of Phase 1) of needs to solution. Once that has been verified, the rep can forecast with greater confidence. Until that point, any rep who forecasts an opportunity based upon a quota-generating sales call and quickly generating a quote is selling on hope and a wish. If the rep does win the deal, he/she may not know the true reason they won it.

All sales reps should be taught the Human Buyer Behavior Model and be able to identify where their prospect is in the process. Forecasts should be based upon where a prospect is in the buying phase, and not upon a sales rep's hunch, or even submitting a proposal. Is the prospect in Phase 1, mapping need to solution? Is the prospect in Phase 2, evaluating the offering in relation to risk and implementation? Is the prospect in Phase 3, where the risk factors have been solved or adequately addressed, and now is in price negotiations?

## Decision Criteria and Outcomes Identified

A sales rep should not give a forecast until he/she is confident the buyer has agreed to the proposed solution in terms of meeting their needs. To prevent excess or bogus forecasting, sales managers can dig into the process of how a sales rep develops a quote. The key information to be obtained is: a) when the buyer's needs or goals have been identified, b) the desired outcome to be received from the solution, and c) the buyer's decision criteria. The rep should know all these facts before the quote is given. As part of an opportunity being identified, to give a higher percentage of certainty, the prospect's buying criteria should be identified. Once those criteria are identified, the seller is in a much better position to know if they can truly deliver and to focus their efforts on meeting that criteria. Knowing the buying criteria and aligning with it greatly increases the chances of winning a deal. In the CRM, one stage should be labeled "Identified Buying Criteria."

I recommend creating a trial quote using bullet points to ensure the buyer agrees to the proposal. I have closed several opportunities based upon trial proposals. I never had to give an official quote, because the buyer agreed to the email and moved ahead with the engagement. All sales forecasting processes should be auditable, that is steps that are clearly identified and completed. The sales manager should be able to see the communication and confirmation of the prospect before a quote is given.

In Phase 2, if the buyer is a mainstream company, they will most likely get other quotes or proposals. It is during this point that the sales rep needs to keep actively adding value with every communication. Remember that the buyer wants an outcome and could care less about a forecast or sales quota. Do not send an email or make a phone call saying, "I'm just checking in to see where you are on the proposal." That is totally seller focused, not Customer Aligned Selling. All communication during every buying phase should have adding value as its purpose. If you know you have added value during Phase 2, then you can increase your forecast percentage.

To get the Phase 3, the buyer must overcome Risk. Where sales managers can help with the forecast is to help the sales rep understand the buyer's risk and make sure the sales rep has asked and documented risk related issues. Too many times a "deal" is forecasted at 75% and then lost because all the issues related to risk were not identified. The sales manager should work with the rep to reduce the risk factors of the prospective buyer.

Many times, opportunities are forecasted at 75%, and a senior level manager tells the rep to cut price to close the deal and meet a quarterly forecast. If risk is the issue that is delaying the sale, then cutting the price just causes the buyer to back up and re-evaluate the offering. By cutting the price when risk is the issue, the buyer is being told that there are truly unidentified risk issues, and the seller knows it; that is why he is cutting the price. When a seller cuts the price when risk is the issue, it can make a buyer mad or very distrustful of the seller.

Here are my recommendations for how a CRM system sales funnel works:

1. New prospect
2. Opportunity identified – need, goal or problem identified
3. Needs analysis- identify desired outcomes, criteria
4. ROI analysis - Solution › Cost
5. Other decision makers identified
6. Identify decision criteria and risks, define success? Evidence need to see?
7. Value proposition/trial proposal
8. Proposal delivered
9. Evaluation phase – identify activities to add value and reduce risk
10. Review of solution – address risk issues
11. Price negotiation
12. Deal closed and won
13. Deal closed and lost

Each of these steps needs to have other fields tied to them so the sales process has an audit trail. When the sales manager asks the rep what he/she did to add value, that activity should be listed in the CRM and tied to the specific stage of the deal. A CRM should have fields that list the customer's buying criteria and risk. If those fields are not filled out, that should be a warning sign for the sales manager. Axiom Sales Force Development has built a Salesforce.com application that has these features. It shows the rep a dashboard of the probability of winning a deal based upon the position of the rep in the account regarding information and decision makers.

Using such methodology in your CRM not only allows you to have better forecasting, it also enables your sales managers to identify the areas in which a particular sales rep needs coaching or skill development. Having an auditable sales process empowers the sales rep to self-diagnose their areas of weakness in an account, or in their skill level, and helps focus the sales manager on developing a specific action plan to improve the chance of winning a deal or improving the sales rep's overall performance. Such a system keeps the sales manager from just saying, "Work harder and/or cut your price to close the deal."

In summary, the key to successful forecasting is to know who the buyers are (technical, financial, and influencers), where the buyers are in the buying process, their decision criteria, and their risk factors. In a complex sale, there are probably many people involved in the decision. Understanding where each person is in the buying process will help a rep know what the next step is for each person, and make for a much more accurate and realistic forecast.

# Epilogue

This has been an overview of how companies buy in the 21ˢᵗ century and what it takes to be an effective sales organization and solution provider. To go deeper into how to sell effectively in the 21ˢᵗ century, I recommend studying, not just reading, these books and courses:

- *Achieve Sales Excellence* by Howard Stevens.
- *Customer Centric Selling 2ⁿᵈ Edition* by Michael Bosworth, John R. Holland and Frank Visgatis
- *Rethinking the Sales Cycle: How Superior Sellers Embrace the Buying Cycle to Achieve a Sustainable and Competitive Advantage* by John R. Holland
- *The Little Teal Book of Trust* by Jeffrey Gitomer
- *Slow Down, Sell Faster* by Kevin Davis
- *The Speed of Trust* by Steven M.R. Covey
- *Cracking the Sales Management Code: The Secrets to Measuring and Managing Sales Performance* by Jason Jordan
- *The Language of Trust: Selling Ideas in a World of Skeptics* by Michael Maslansky

Read the sales research coming out of such fine institutions as the University of Houston Sales Excellence Institute (http://www.bauer.uh.edu/sei/h). One of their lead researchers is Michael Aherne, Ph.D. You can access his research via his university web page.

The Schey Sales Center at Ohio University is another excellent source for research (http://www.thesalescentre.com/).), as well as

Indiana University's Center for Global Sales Leadership (http://kelley. iu.edu/globalsales/). Other notable schools that have outstanding sales curriculum are DePaul, Kennesaw State University, and Florida State University.

To learn more about hiring students with a degree in sales or a sales certification, or find the top schools in these areas, visit the Sales Education Foundation website at http://salesfoundation.org/resources/.

# Notes

1) Howard Stevens and Theodore Kinni, *Achieve Sales Excellence,* (Avon, MA: Penguin Press, 2007)

2) Jeffrey Gitomer, *The Little Teal Book of Trust, How to earn it, grow it, and keep it to become a trusted advisor in sales, business and life.* (Upper Saddle River, NJ: FT Press, 2008)

3) Jeffery Gitomer, *The Little Red Book of Selling,* (Austin, TX: Bard Press, 2005)

4) Jeffrey Gitomer, *The Little Black Book of Connections, 6.5 Assets for Networking Your Way to Rich Relationships,* (Austin, TX: Bard Press, 2006)

5) David H. Sandler and John Haynes, PhD, *You Can't Teach a Kid to Ride a Bike at a Seminar: The Sandler Sales Institute 7 Step System for Successful Selling,* (New York, NY: Penguin Press, 1996)

6) Billy Cox, *The All Star Sales Book, Get in the Game, Boost Your Numbers and Earn the Big Bucks,* (Austin, TX: Greenleaf Book Press, 2008)

7) Matthew Dixon and Brent Adamson, *The Challenger Sales: Taking Control of the Customer Conversation,* (New York, NY; Penguin Group, 2011)

8) Kevin Davis, *Slow Down and Sell Faster, Understand Your Customer's Buying Process and Maximize Your Sales,* (New York, NY: AMACON, 2011)

9) Keith Rosen, *Coaching Sales People into Sales Champions, a Tactical Playbook for Managers and Executives,* (Hoboken, NJ: John Wiley & Sons, 2008)

10) Steven M.R. Covoy, *The Speed of Trust: The One Thing That Changes Everything,* (New York, NY: Free Press, 2006)

11) Michael T. Bosworth, John R. Holland and Frank Visgatis, *Customer Centric Selling, Second Edition,* (Columbus, OH: McGraw-Hill Publishing, 2010)

12) John R. Holland, *Rethinking the Sales Cycle: How Superior Sellers Embrace the Buying Cycle to Achieve a Sustainable and Competitive Advantage,* (Columbus, OH: McGraw-Hill Publishing, 2008)

13) Orrin Woodward, *Resolved, 13 Resolutions for Life,* (Flint, MI: Obstacles Press, 2011)

14) Daniel H. Pink, *A Whole New Mind -Why Right Brainers Will Rule the Future,* (New York, NY, Riverhead, 2006)

15) Bunnell Idea Group, *Grow Big, The Art of Non-Sales* Course, The Path to a Raving Fan module, pp 6-7 (Atlanta, GA)

16) Jason Jordan and Michelle Vazzana, *Cracking the Sales Management Code: The Secrets to Measuring and Managing Sales Performance,* (Columbus, OH: McGraw-Hill Publishing 2012)

# Bonus · What Really Drives You?

This is my personal story and involves the topic of life motives and faith. I have shared my story in hopes that it may help others experience what I have.

In life, everyone has something that drives them and gives them meaning and a reason to exist. For most people, there are two sources of energy; one is positive and the other is negative. Your driving energy is either derived from strength and love or from fear and control. Your energy is what controls how you think, what you will do, and how you interpret situations.

If you are driven from strength and love, you can see life experiences in a positive manner and focus on how you can serve others, and make life better for yourself and others. If you are driven from the energy of fear and control, then your actions are designed to protect you and control your environment. The roots of your actions are very self-centered and negative. Fear and the need for control zap you of positive energy to move forward in life, to grow, and to serve others. Fear and control can cause you to be focused on image management and not enjoy just being yourself.

I want to share what drives me.

My passion for serving the customer comes from strength and love. What gives me that strength and love? It is my faith in a God who loves me, cares for me, and was even willing to die for me that I might live.

I believe that the Bible is true and what it says about mankind is true: that all men and women are sinful beings, alienated from the glory they were created to be a part of. In the book of Romans, the Apostle Paul writes that "All have sinned and fall short of the glory of God." This separation from God is because we do evil things, have evil thoughts, and can never, no matter how hard we try, become perfect. Paul also wrote, "There is none righteous, no not one." (Romans 3:10) So, we are separated from God and our desire to live in strength and love is distorted, and we live a life motivated by fear and control.

God provided an answer to our condition in terms of a free gift. He sent his Son, Jesus of Nazareth, a real person who lived in Israel between 4 BC and 30 AD, to die for our sins. Jesus was not just a good man; he claimed to be God in the flesh. The gospel accounts of Matthew, Mark, and Luke have this story of Jesus' immaculate birth, his life, his claims to be God, and his horrible death on a Roman cross. In the book of John, Jesus makes this claim: "I am the way, the truth and the life. No one comes to the Father except through me." Jesus is saying that He is the only way to heaven. There is no other.

The book of Hebrews in the New Testament portion of the Bible explains that a righteous and just God must require punishment for sin; otherwise he would not be just and righteous. That punishment means that you and I, because of our sin, will receive death. But this God also loves his creation so much that he chose to offer a gift of salvation. He prepared a way out of our desperate situation. He chose to have his son die for the penalty of our sins, yours and mine: a righteous man, Jesus, dying for the unrighteous, you and me. Romans 6:23 states, "For the wages of sin are death, but the free gift of God is eternal life in Christ Jesus our Lord." To prove that Jesus truly conquered death and that we can have eternal life, Jesus rose from the dead and was seen by 500 people. He then ascended into Heaven while in the midst of a group of people.[11] This was no myth for there were over 500 witnesses, and his

---

[11] From the Bible- the Book of Acts 9:1-11.

twelve apostles were willing to be tortured and die for their belief in Jesus! These very witnesses wrote the New Testament, sharing not only their story, but God's plan of redemption.

This Jesus offers you and me the gift of eternal life. It is just that: a gift. You cannot earn eternal life, but you can receive it. Paul wrote in Romans 10:9-10, "If you confess with your mouth that Jesus is Lord and believe in your heart that God raised him from the dead, you will be saved. For with the heart one believes and is justified (made right with God) and with the mouth one confesses and is saved." This gift is what is called God's grace. Grace is unmerited or undeserved mercy. You must receive this grace as a gift, for God's favor cannot be earned.

Receiving this gift is a simple as saying and believing, "Jesus, I am a sinner and cannot save myself. I live my life in fear and control. Please come into my life and save me from myself. Grant me eternal life."

If you receive this gift, eternal life does not begin when you die, but begins immediately. Jesus gives you a new life now, a life that can be lived through strength and love, not fear and control. 2 Corinthians 5:17 says, "If anyone is in Christ, he is a new creation; the old is gone and the new is come." Jesus said in John 10:10, "The thief comes to kill and destroy. I have come that they may have life and have it abundantly." So, if you are not a believer in Jesus, living in fear and control is normal, knowing that the thief, that is Satan or the Devil, (yes, even Jesus says he exists and is evil)[12], is seeking to kill and destroy you. But, with the power and new life that you can have in and through Jesus Christ, you can have an abundant life living in strength and love.

Today is day of choice. You may not have known what I just shared. Now you know. Ask yourself, "Are my motivations in life driven by fear and the need for control?" "Do I want to change? Do I want peace?" If yes, ask Jesus into your life and receive his free gift of salvation, and his grace to you. Then he can begin to change your heart and mind

---

[12] John 8:43-44 and Matthew 12:24-28

from one of fear and control, to living in strength and love. Jesus said in John 14:27, "Peace I leave with you; my peace I give to you. Not as the world gives do I give to you. Let not your hearts be troubled, neither let them be afraid." The peace and living a life in strength and love comes through the transformation of your mind. Paul says in Romans 12:2, "Be not conformed to the pattern of this world but be transformed by the renewing of your mind so that you may test and approve the will of God, his good and perfect will."

If you made this decision today, congratulations! You are now part of a worldwide group in which the apostles of Jesus called the body of Christ, or Christians. Go share this good news with someone. To read more on the life of Jesus, get a Bible, or go to www.biblegateway.com or download the Bible app from Google Play Store or Apple. I suggest you begin with the book of John.

To understand more about living in the freedom of God's grace, you may contact me or Google search "God's grace." You may also read books by Timothy Keller or John Stott. Two great sites that teach that your life is transformed by truly believing and living in grace are:

1) My church, Oak Mountain Presbyterian http://ompc.org/connect. Listen to one of the sermons on God's grace.
2) Another great teacher is Kerry Shook, http://kerryshook.org/.

Blessings to you,
Bill Hart

Printed in the United States
By Bookmasters